PROSE FICTION

Prose Fiction

An Introduction to the Semiotics of Narrative

Ignasi Ribó

https://www.openbookpublishers.com/

© 2019 Ignasi Ribó

This work is licensed under a Creative Commons Attribution 4.0 International license (CC BY 4.0). This license allows you to share, copy, distribute and transmit the work; to adapt the work and to make commercial use of the work providing attribution is made to the author (but not in any way that suggests that they endorse you or your use of the work).

Attribution should include the following information:

Ignasi Ribó, *Prose Fiction: An Introduction to the Semiotics of Narrative*. Cambridge, UK: Open Book Publishers, 2019. https://doi.org/10.11647/OBP.0187

In order to access detailed and updated information on the license, please visit https://doi.org/10.11647/OBP.0187#copyright

Further details about CC BY licenses are available at http://creativecommons.org/licenses/by/4.0/

All external links were active at the time of publication unless otherwise stated and have been archived via the Internet Archive Wayback Machine at https://archive.org/web

Any digital material and resources associated with this volume are available at https://doi.org/10.11647/OBP.0187#resources

Every effort has been made to identify and contact copyright holders and any omission or error will be corrected if notification is made to the publisher.

ISBN Paperback: 978-1-78374-809-9
ISBN Hardback: 978-1-78374-810-5
ISBN Digital (PDF): 978-1-78374-811-2
ISBN Digital ebook (epub): 978-1-78374-812-9
ISBN Digital ebook (mobi): 978-1-78374-813-6
ISBN Digital (XML): 978-1-78374-814-3
DOI: 10.11647/OBP.0187

Cover image: Photo by chuttersnap on Unsplash at https://unsplash.com/photos/AG2Ct_DqCh0

Cover design: Anna Gatti

Contents

About the Author — vii
Acknowledgements — ix

Preface — xi

1. **Introduction** — 1
   1.1 What Is Narrative? — 2
   1.2 Genres — 4
   1.3 Prose Fiction — 6
   1.4 Story and Discourse — 9
   1.5 Beyond Literature — 11
   Summary — 13
   References — 14

2. **Plot** — 17
   2.1 The Thread of Narrative — 18
   2.2 Emplotment — 20
   2.3 Beginnings, Middles, and Ends — 22
   2.4 Conflict and Resolution — 26
   2.5 Suspense and Surprise — 29
   Summary — 30
   References — 31

3. **Setting** — 33
   3.1 The World of Narrative — 34
   3.2 Topography and Atmosphere — 36
   3.3 Kinds of Setting — 38
   3.4 Description — 40
   3.5 Verisimilitude — 42
   Summary — 44
   References — 45

4. **Characterisation** — 47
   4.1 The Actants of Narrative — 49
   4.2 Individuation — 50
   4.3 Kinds of Character — 54

	4.4 Representing Characters	57
	4.5 Dialogue	60
	Summary	62
	References	62
5.	**Narration**	**65**
	5.1 The Expression of Narrative	66
	5.2 Narrators and Narratees	68
	5.3 Focalisation	71
	5.4 Telling and Showing	74
	5.5 Commentary	76
	Summary	78
	References	79
6.	**Language**	**81**
	6.1 The Style of Narrative	82
	6.2 Foregrounding	84
	6.3 Figures of Speech	86
	6.4 Symbolism	89
	6.5 Translation	91
	Summary	93
	References	93
7.	**Theme**	**95**
	7.1 The Meaning of Narrative	96
	7.2 Identity	98
	7.3 Ideology	101
	7.4 Morality	103
	7.5 Art and Politics	105
	Summary	106
	References	107

Bibliography	109
Illustrations	113
Examples of Short Stories and Novels	119
Glossary of Narrative Terms	135

About the Author

Ignasi Ribó (Ph.D. in Modern European Literature and Thought, University of Sussex) is a Catalan writer and scholar. He has been teaching Literary Theory and Semiotics at university level for more than ten years and currently works as a Lecturer in the School of Liberal Arts at Mae Fah Luang University (Chiang Rai, Thailand). Ignasi is the author of several novels, as well as academic essays on literary theory, comparative literature, ecocriticism, biosemiotics, cultural ecology, and environmental philosophy. More information on the author's website: https://www.ignasiribo.com

Acknowledgements

I would like to thank the School of Liberal Arts at Mae Fah Luang University (MFU) for giving me the opportunity to teach the 'Short Stories and Novels' course to English-major third-year students. This textbook was specifically written for this course and would probably have never seen the light of day, at least in this form, if I had not been assigned this task.

In particular, I would like to thank the coordinator of the course, Ajarn Teeranuch Anurit, as well as Ajarn Panida Monyanont and Ajarn Khanisara Sirisit, who taught this and other literary courses with me at MFU. It was an enjoyable and rewarding experience being part of this literature team.

I would also like to thank my English major students, who mostly came from Thailand, but in some cases also from Korea, Japan, China, Bhutan, and Myanmar, for their interest and willingness to learn the basics of narrative theory, especially considering that most of them had limited experience in literary studies before attending MFU. This book was written for them and for many other students like them who might be interested in studying this subject elsewhere.

I also want to thank the anonymous reviewers who contributed to improving the quality of the book with their insightful comments and suggestions during the peer review process.

Finally, I would like to thank Alessandra Tosi and the editorial team at Open Book Publishers for believing in this textbook and making it available to readers and students around the world. At a time when the publishing industry tends to look at its bottom line more than at the lines it prints, it is a truly commendable enterprise to produce high-quality academic books that can be accessed, read and used by everyone free of charge.

Preface

This book is a college-level introduction to the concepts of narrative theory (or narratology) that students need in order to develop their competence in analysing, interpreting and writing prose fiction.

The book has been conceived and written for undergraduate students majoring in English literature and language, as well as in other disciplines of the Humanities, in Asia. In general, Asian students have only had a limited exposure to Western literature and literary theories during their high-school education. The book aims to provide an easy-to-follow introduction for these students, giving them the tools to read and engage in critical discussion of narrative texts without burdening them with excessive historical or theoretical details. The book should also be useful to Western students, either at high-school or college-level, as well as to general readers interested in learning more about the literary devices used in narrative texts, particularly in prose fiction genres such as short stories and novels.

Prose Fiction presents the most important concepts of narratology in a rigorous but accessible way. It follows a semiotic model of narrative communication, which is based on the most recent literary theory, but avoids engaging in overtly technical debates. By using simple language and relying on many examples drawn from a wide range of short stories and novels, some of them well-known to students, the book allows them to develop a thorough understanding of the key elements of narrative.

This material is intended to be used as the main textbook in a syllabus that would also include a selection of readings, and in-class interpretation and discussion of stories drawn from a variety of authors, genres and periods. It can also be used as a supplementary textbook in creative writing courses, especially those focused on narrative fiction.

The book begins by introducing the 'semiotic model of narrative,' which incorporates key elements of narratological theory into a single coherent framework. The different elements of this framework are then

© Ignasi Ribó, CC BY 4.0   https://doi.org/10.11647/OBP.0187.08

developed in subsequent chapters. This structure allows the student to progressively develop a comprehensive understanding of narrative without getting lost in the intricacies of theory.

The initial chapters on plot, setting and characterisation are particularly important for a narratological analysis of stories. They constitute the most accessible part of the book, providing plenty of examples that allow students to better understand the key concepts presented. More challenging, but also important from a narratological perspective, is the chapter on narration. The following two chapters, on language and theme, are not usually covered so extensively by most textbooks on narrative. The chapter on language explores figurative devices generally used in prose fiction, and is particularly useful for students who are not familiar with rhetoric. Finally, the chapter on theme incorporates perspectives drawn from contemporary critical theory (feminism, postcolonialism, etc.) that are not generally discussed in similar textbooks but constitute an essential aspect of contemporary literary criticism.

The language used in the book is purposely simple and accessible to undergraduate students without previous knowledge of literature. Key concepts are defined in the glossary at the end of the book. Throughout the text, an effort is made to systematically classify and structure the different elements of narrative in ways that facilitate understanding and retention by students.

I have purposefully avoided giving specific text samples or readings, because I believe that instructors should feel free to design their own reading list, based on their own interests and knowledge, as well as on their students' preferences and the context of their teaching. I see this textbook as a bare-bones presentation of narrative theory. The book provides a conceptual skeleton, allowing teachers to decide what flesh they want to add, in order to construct a working model for an effective course on the anatomy of fiction.

Given the abstract nature of many of the concepts discussed, I have tried to provide examples throughout the book. These examples are not developed in detail and are solely used to illustrate key concepts and make them easier to understand for students. They also aim to provide a sense of the diversity, complexity and excitement of fiction narratives. While the examples are drawn from a wide variety of short stories and novels, including both classical and popular fiction from different languages and cultures, most of the texts were originally written in English. This predominance of English (or rather, English-language) literature can be explained in part because the textbook was originally written for students majoring in English language and literature. But it also reflects the current status of English as the preeminent global language, a fact which necessarily affects the international projection of its literature. Coming from a country whose language and culture have been historically minoritised, I am nonetheless quite sensitive to the negative consequences that derive from the supremacy of the English language. Thus, I have tried my best to expand the cultural range of examples in order to reflect the rich diversity of world literature.

However, I am not entirely sure if I have succeeded in this effort, and most likely my explanations and examples are too heavily determined by the European tradition, which is, after all, my own. In any case, at the end of the book, I have provided a short summary and contextualisation of all the stories that I use as examples. Each entry also includes a link to additional sources of information (i.e., Wikipedia), in order to guide students in their own exploration of the literary canon beyond the formal classroom reading list.

While the textbook necessarily reflects my own biases and shortcomings, I hope that it will spark the interest of students in literary narratives, encouraging them to read more, but above all, to read more critically.

Chiang Rai, 1 October 2019

1. Introduction

In one form or another, stories are part of everyone's lives. We are constantly telling each other stories, usually about events that happen to us or to people we know. These are usually not invented stories, but they are stories nonetheless. And we would not be able to make sense of our world and our lives without them.

We also enjoy reading, watching, or listening to stories that we know are not true, but whose characters, places, and events spark our imagination and allow us to experience different worlds as if they were our own. These are the kind of stories we call 'fiction.' Many people like to watch series or soap operas on TV. And even more people like to watch movies, whether in the cinema or streamed to their laptop or smartphone. Video games, comics and manga, songs and musicals, stage plays, and YouTube blogs, they all tell stories in their own ways. But if there is one medium that has shown itself particularly well-suited to tell engaging and lasting stories throughout the ages, it is written language. It is fair to say, then, that stories, and most particularly fictions, in their various forms and genres, constitute the backbone of literature.

In this chapter, we will introduce some basic ideas about storytelling, and in particular about the narrative forms of literature and the ways in which they create meaning. We will also present the main genres into which literary narratives have been divided historically, and how these genres have evolved from their origins until today. We will then try to define and frame the two genres of prose fiction that are more common nowadays and from which we will draw the examples in this textbook: short stories and novels.

Not everyone approaches these genres in the same way. Here, we will follow a semiotic model to study and interpret narrative structure and meaning. In order to understand this model, it is essential to grasp the distinction between story and discourse, which will guide our discussions throughout the book. To conclude this chapter, we will consider how short stories and novels spread beyond the written word and become interconnected with other media in contemporary culture.

© Ignasi Ribó, CC BY 4.0   https://doi.org/10.11647/OBP.0187.01

1.1 What Is Narrative?

Narrative is notoriously difficult to define with precision. But even before we attempt a working definition of the concept, we already know that it refers to storytelling. The term itself comes from the Latin word *narro*, which means 'to tell.' In English, to narrate means to tell a story. According to many anthropologists, this ability is universal amongst human beings.[1] All peoples, everywhere and throughout history, tell each other stories, or, as they are technically called, narratives. As the semiotician and literary critic Roland Barthes once wrote,

> The narratives of the world are numberless. Narrative is first and foremost a prodigious variety of genres, themselves distributed amongst different substances — as though any material were fit to receive man's stories. Able to be carried by articulated language, spoken or written, fixed or moving images, gestures, and the ordered mixture of all these substances; narrative is present in myth, legend, fable, tale, novella, epic, history, tragedy, drama, comedy, mime, painting, stained-glass windows, cinema, comics, news items, conversation. Moreover, under this almost infinite diversity of forms, narrative is present in every age, in every place, in every society; it begins with the very history of mankind and there has never been a people without narrative. All classes, all human groups, have their narratives, enjoyment of which is very often shared by men with different, even opposing, cultural backgrounds. Caring nothing for the division between good and bad literature, narrative is international, transhistorical, transcultural: it is simply there, like life itself.[2]

For the purpose of this book, we will define narrative as the semiotic representation of a sequence of events, meaningfully connected by time and cause.[3] This definition highlights certain key elements shared by all forms of narrative:

1. Narratives are *semiotic representations*, that is, they are made of material signs (written or spoken words, moving or still images, etc.) which convey or stand for meanings that need to be decoded or interpreted by the receiver.

2. Narratives present a *sequence of events*, that is, they connect at least two events (actions, happenings, incidents, etc.) in a common structure or organised whole.

---

[1] See, for example, William Bascom, 'The Forms of Folklore: Prose Narratives,' *The Journal of American Folklore*, 78:307 (1965), 3–20.

[2] Roland Barthes, 'Introduction to the Structural Analysis of Narrative,' in *A Roland Barthes Reader*, ed. by Susan Sontag, trans. by Stephen Heath (London: Vintage, 1994), pp. 251–52.

[3] Based on *Narratology: An Introduction*, ed. by Susana Onega Jaén and José Angel García Landa (London: Routledge, 1996), p. 3, https://doi.org/10.4324/9781315843018

3. Narratives connect events by *time and cause*, that is, they organise the sequence of events based on their relationship in time ('Hear the sweet cuckoo. Through the big-bamboo thicket, the full moon filters.'[4]), as cause and effect ('Into the old pond, a frog suddenly plunges. The sound of water.'[5]), or, in most narratives, by both temporal and causal relationships.

4. Narratives are *meaningful*, that is, they have meaning for both senders and receivers, although these meanings do not need to be the same.

As this definition suggests, narrative is the fundamental way in which we humans make sense of our existence. Without effort, we connect everything that happens in our lifeworld (events) as a temporal or causal sequence, and most often as both. In order to understand our lives and the world around us, we need to tell ourselves and each other meaningful stories. Even our perception of things that appear to be static inevitably involves making up stories.[6] Are you able to look at the picture in Figure 1.1 below without seeing a connected sequence of events, a narrative, in it?

Fig. 1.1 Collision of Costa Concordia, cropped (2012). By Roberto Vongher, CC BY-SA 3.0, https://commons.wikimedia.org/wiki/File:Collision_of_Costa_Concordia_5_crop.jpg

---

4   Haiku by Matsuo Bashō, in Daniel Crump Buchanan, *One Hundred Famous Haiku* (Tokyo: Japan Publications, 1973), p. 87.
5   Haiku by Matsuo Bashō, in Buchanan, p. 88.
6   H. Porter Abbott, *The Cambridge Introduction to Narrative* (Cambridge, UK: Cambridge University Press, 2008), https://doi.org/10.1017/cbo9780511816932

1.2 Genres

Genres are conventional groupings of texts (or other semiotic representations) based on certain shared features. These groupings, which have been used since ancient times by writers, readers, and critics, serve a variety of functions:

1. *Classification*: By identifying the features that are worthy of attention, genres help us to place a particular text among similar texts and distinguish it from most other texts.
2. *Prescription*: Genres institute standards and rules that guide writers in their work. Sometimes these rules are actively enforced (normative genres), while at other times they act simply as established customs.
3. *Interpretation*: These same standards and rules help readers to interpret texts, by providing them with shared conventions and expectations about the different texts they might encounter.
4. *Evaluation*: Critics also use these standards and rules when they set about judging the artistic quality of a text, by comparing it with other texts in the same genre.

Already in Ancient Greece and Rome, narrative was a major literary genre (*epic*), distinct from poetic song (*lyric*) and stage performance (*drama*). Other generic classifications, particularly those related to the content of the story (tragedy, comedy, pastoral, satire, etc.), were also commonly used. But the basic classification of poetic forms at the time, established by Plato and Aristotle, was based on whether the poet told the story (*diegesis*) or the story was represented or imitated by actors (*mimesis*).

While Classical and Neoclassical poetics thought of genres as fixed and preordained forms that poets needed to abide by, modern literary theory, starting with the Romantic period, has come to see genres as dynamic and loosely defined conventions. Genres change and evolve through time. Different cultures define and institute different genres. In fact, modern literature has seen a significant expansion of genres, as a visit to any bookstore or online bookseller will attest (see Fig. 1.2).

Genres are continuously evolving across many different dimensions, such as content, style, form, etc. They are often organised at different levels of subordination, in hierarchies or taxonomies of genres and subgenres. Nowadays, for example, the following generic distinctions are commonly used to classify stories:

1. Fiction vs. nonfiction (based on whether the events and the characters of the story are invented or taken from reality).

Fig. 1.2 El Ateneo Gran Splendid. A theatre converted into a bookshop. Buenos Aires, Argentina. Photo by Galio, CC BY-SA 3.0, https://commons.wikimedia.org/wiki/File:Buenos_Aires_-_Recoleta_-_El_Ateneo_ex_Grand_Splendid_2.JPG

2. Prose vs. verse (based on the literary technique used to tell the story).
3. Narrative vs. drama (based on whether the story is told or shown).
4. Novel, novella, or short story (based on the length of the story).
5. Adventure, fantasy, romance, humour, science-fiction, crime, etc. (based on the content of the story).

These and many other generic classifications allow us to impose some order on the vast number of stories that are published every year. But they are not set in stone and are certainly not eternal. Following the disposition of writers, readers, and critics, new genres appear and disappear, often combining the characteristics of previous texts or developing from the ambiguous boundaries of existing genres, as with the blending of 'fact' and 'fiction' into 'faction' (or nonfiction novel).[7] There is little doubt that novels and short stories are the most popular narrative fiction genres in contemporary literature. Like all genres, however, they appeared at some point in history and will only last as long as people are interested in writing and reading them.

---

7   See David Lodge, *The Art of Fiction: Illustrated from Classic and Modern Texts* (New York, NY: Viking, 1993), p. 203.

1.3 Prose Fiction

Prose is text written or spoken with the pattern of ordinary or everyday language, without a metrical structure. Verse, on the other hand, is written or spoken with an arranged metrical rhythm, and often a rhyme. While narrative fiction composed in verse was very common in the past, modern writers overwhelmingly tell their stories in prose, to the point that most readers today would be baffled if they encountered fiction written in verse.

By far, the most popular genres of prose fiction nowadays are novels and short stories. The distinction between the two is fairly simple and straightforward: short stories are short, novels are long. Any other difference that we might be able to find between these two genres of narrative is derived in one way or another from this simple fact.

But before identifying certain key differences, it is important to understand that both short stories and novels are modern narrative genres, which only emerged in their current forms during the European Renaissance.[8] Of course, people had been telling each other fictional stories in other forms since much earlier and in many other places. Perhaps the two forms that had the strongest influence on the emergence of these modern genres of prose fiction were the Classical epic poems, most particularly Homer's *Iliad* and *Odyssey*, and the Hebrew Bible, which is filled with a wide variety of short stories.

During the European Renaissance, these and other influences stimulated many writers to produce fictional narratives in prose using vernacular languages (instead of Latin), so that they could reach a growing audience of readers. These narratives were not intended to be read aloud, like epic poems or other forms of poetry and drama, but silently, as part of an intimate experience between the reader and the text.[9] Initially, these new narratives, inspired in Middle Eastern and Indian storytelling, tended to be short and were often published as a collection, like Giovanni Boccaccio's *Decameron* (1353, Fig. 1.3). Contemporaries referred to them as *novelle* (singular, *novella*), which means 'new' in Italian and is a term still in use today to refer to short novels. From the perspective of Western culture, these early *novelle* are the first modern forms of prose fiction.

A little later in the Renaissance, some authors began to extend these *novelle* into longer stories that occupied the whole book with the adventures of a single protagonist. In this way, what we now call the novel was born. The first modern novel, according to most, is Miguel de Cervantes' *Don Quixote* (1605, Fig. 1.4), the tragicomic story of a deluded country squire who tries to revive the heroic lifestyle depicted in fictional books

---

8   For a detailed history, see Paul Cobley, *Narrative* (London, UK: Routledge, 2014).
9   Alberto Manguel, *A History of Reading* (New York, NY: Penguin Books, 2014).

Fig. 1.3
Boccaccio, *Decameron*: 'The Story of the Marchioness of Montferrat,' 15th century. Bibliothèque nationale de France, Public Domain, https://commons.wikimedia.org/wiki/File:Decameron_BNF_MS_Italien_63_f_22v.jpeg

of chivalry. We should not forget, however, that long narratives, similar in many ways to modern novels, had already been written and read in different cultures throughout history. For example, Lucius Apuleius' *The Golden Ass* (ca. 170), Longus' *Daphnis and Chloe* (2nd century), Murasaki Shikibu's *Tale of Genji* (1010), Ramon Llull's *Blanquerna* (1283), or Luo Guanzhong's *Romance of the Three Kingdoms* (ca. 1321), amongst many others.

Due to their difference in length, short stories and novels also tend to differ from each other in certain respects:

- Short stories need to focus on a few characters, a limited number of environments, and just one sequence of events. They cannot afford to digress or add unnecessary complications to the plot. Density, concentration, and precision are essential elements of good short-story writing.

- Novels, on the other hand, can explore many different characters, environments, and events. The story can be enriched with subplots and complications that add perspective, dynamism, and interest to the novel. Characters have room to evolve and the author can introduce digressions and commentary without undermining the form. Scope, breadth, and sweep are essential elements of good novel writing.

Fig. 1.4. Title page of the first edition of Miguel de Cervantes' *Don Quixote* (1605). Biblioteca Digital Hispánica, Public Domain, https://en.wikipedia.org/wiki/Don_Quixote#/media/File:El_ingenioso_hidalgo_don_Quijote_de_la_Mancha.jpg

This does not mean that the novel is better or worse than the short story. They are simply different forms of narrative, both well adapted to achieve their own purposes. While the novel can recreate a fictional world in all its complexity and vastness, the short story is able to shine a sharper light on a particular character or situation.

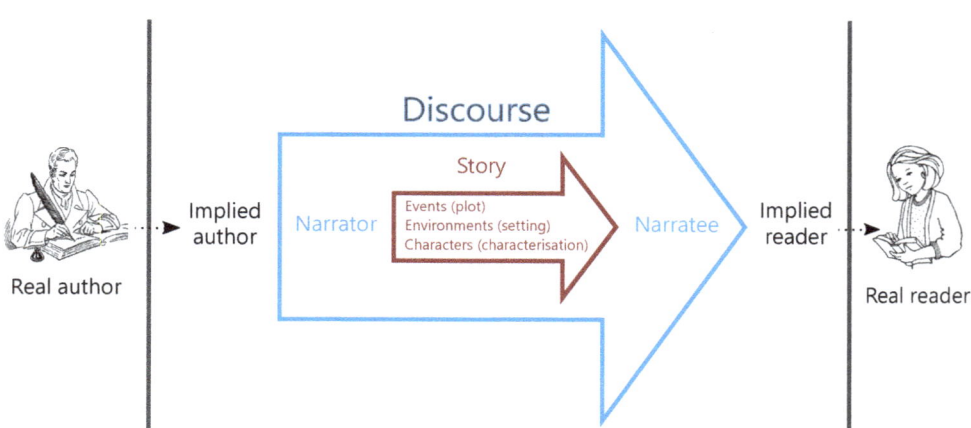

Fig. 1.5 Semiotic model of narrative. By Ignasi Ribó, CC BY.

1.4 Story and Discourse

The systematic study of narratives in order to understand their structure (how they work) and function (what they are for) is called narratology.[10] This field has developed a set of conceptual tools that allow us to discern with more clarity and precision the process through which narratives are meaningful for writers and readers. Narratology is closely linked with semiotics, the study of meaning-making processes, and in particular the use of signs and signifying systems to communicate meanings. In this sense, it is important to realise that narratological models are not so much concerned with explaining individual narratives, but rather they attempt to identify the underlying semiotic system that makes narrative production and reception possible.[11]

The semiotic or communicative model of narrative that will be developed in this textbook (see Fig. 1.5) begins by distinguishing the real people who participate in the communicative act of writing and reading (the real author and the real reader) from their textual or implied counterparts.

Thus, the 'implied author'[12] is not the actual individual who wrote the book, but a projection of that individual in the book itself. For instance, Ernest Hemingway (Fig. 1.6) was born in 1899, wrote novels like *The Old Man and the Sea* and short stories like 'The Snows of Kilimanjaro,' and died in 1961. When we read one of his narratives, we are not listening to him telling us a story (how could we?), but to a virtual persona to whom we can attribute a style, attitudes, and values, based on what we find in the text itself.

Similarly, although we are the actual readers, the text does not address us as particular individuals. Otherwise, every book could only have a single intended receiver and the rest of us would be eavesdroppers. But books, unlike letters, are generally addressed to an abstract or generic receiver. We can define the notion of 'implied reader'[13] as the virtual persona to whom the implied author is addressing the narrative, as can be deduced from the text itself. When anyone of us, at any time, picks up a Hemingway novel or short story and starts to read it, we are effectively stepping into the shoes of its implied reader.

---

10   See Mieke Bal, *Narratology: Introduction to the Theory of Narrative* (Toronto: University of Toronto Press, 2017).

11   David Herman, *Basic Elements of Narrative* (Chichester, UK: Wiley-Blackwell, 2009), https://doi.org/10.1002/9781444305920; Jørgen Dines Johansen, *Literary Discourse: A Semiotic-Pragmatic Approach to Literature* (Toronto: University of Toronto Press, 2002), https://doi.org/10.3138/9781442676725

12   Wayne C. Booth, *The Rhetoric of Fiction* (Chicago, IL: University of Chicago Press, 1983).

13   Wolfgang Iser, *The Implied Reader: Patterns of Communication in Prose Fiction from Bunyan to Beckett* (Baltimore, MD: Johns Hopkins University Press, 1995).

Fig. 1.6
Ernest Hemingway posing for a dust-jacket photo by Lloyd Arnold for the first edition of *For Whom the Bell Tolls* (1940), at Sun Valley Lodge, Idaho, 1939. By Lloyd Arnold, Public Domain, https://en.wikipedia.org/wiki/File:ErnestHemingway.jpg

Once we move into the narrative text itself, which already contains an implied author and an implied reader, both only circumstantially related to human beings in the real world, we need to distinguish two different levels of communication: *discourse* and *story*.[14]

At one level, there is the message that the implied author sends to the implied reader. We will call this message 'discourse.' Narrative discourse is the means through which the narrative is communicated by the implied author to the implied reader. It includes elements like:

- Narration (narrator and narratee, point of view, etc.)
- Language
- Theme

The content of narrative discourse is a 'story.' But the story is not told directly by the implied author to the implied reader. It is the narrator (a figure of discourse) who tells the story to a narratee (another figure of discourse). Sometimes, narrators and narratees are also characters in the story, but at other times they are not. Therefore, we cannot say that narrators or narratees are people, nor even characters. Both exist only in narrative discourse. The story, then, is simply what the narrator communicates to the narratee (see Fig. 1.7). It includes elements like:

---

14 See Seymour Benjamin Chatman, *Reading Narrative Fiction* (New York, NY: Macmillan, 1993); Seymour Benjamin Chatman, *Story and Discourse: Narrative Structure in Fiction and Film* (Ithaca, NY: Cornell University Press, 2000).

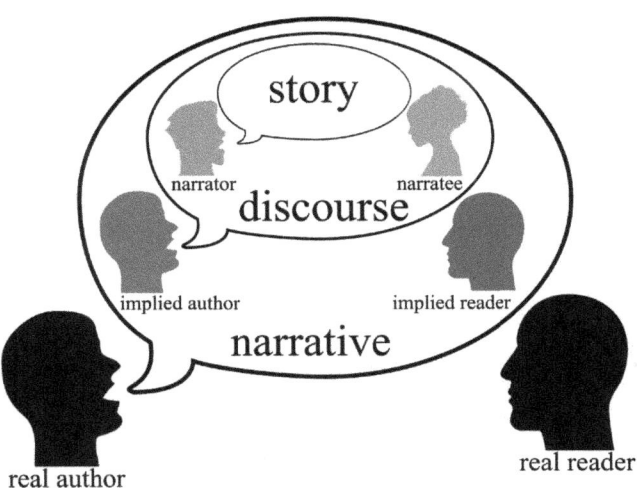

Fig. 1.7 Semiotic model of narrative shown in speech bubbles. By Ignasi Ribó, CC BY.

- Events (plot)
- Environments (setting)
- Characters (characterisation)

In the next chapters, we will examine all these elements in more detail. First, we will look at the key elements of story: plot, setting, and characterisation. Then, we will examine the key elements of discourse: narration, language, and theme. While reading these chapters it is important to keep in mind the fundamental distinction between story and discourse, without which many aspects of narrative fiction cannot be properly understood.

1.5 Beyond Literature

As we have seen, narratives are not confined to literary works. Certainly, novels and short stories have been the privileged vehicles of storytelling since the European Renaissance until the present day. But the invention of other media, such as cinema, television, or the Internet, has been rapidly changing the way people produce and consume narratives.

During the twentieth century, cinema developed into an alternative medium to tell the kind of stories that previously were the domain of novels or plays. Like novels, movies are narratives that present a sequence of events connected by time and cause. Unlike novels, however, movies are not meant to be read, but to be watched. In this sense, movies are like theatre plays: they show a performance of the events, environments, and characters of the story, rather than having a narrator convey those events, environments, and characters through words. Of course, cinema is not completely like drama, because the camera, by selecting and framing the events presented in the narrative, acts in some ways like a narrator. In fact, we may well consider cinema a new narrative form, one that draws both from the epic (prose fiction) and dramatic (stage play) genres.[15]

The intimate relationship between literary and cinematographic narratives is clearly shown by the fact that many movies have tried to retell the stories found in prose fiction. In general, a narrative based on a story previously presented in a different medium is called an adaptation. In some cases, prose fictions are also adaptations, for example when they take their stories from journalistic accounts, history books, or even movies. Much more common, however, is for movies to attempt to bring successful novels and short stories to the screen. For example, J. K. Rowling's series of novels about the adventures of the young wizard Harry Potter and his friends has been adapted into popular movies by Hollywood (see Fig. 1.8). Television has also drawn many of its fictions from literary narratives. One example is the adaptation of George R. R. Martin's series of medieval fantasy novels *A Song of Ice and Fire* into a successful television show, *Game of Thrones*.

Fig. 1.8 Warner Bros. Studio Tour London: The Making of Harry Potter. Photo by Karen Roe, CC BY 2.0, https://commons.wikimedia.org/wiki/File:The_Making_of_Harry_Potter_29-05-2012_(7528990230).jpg

Adaptations are always the subject of passionate debate and controversy. Many attempts to adapt great novels to cinema or television have been

---

15   See Robert Stam, *Film Theory: An Introduction* (Malden, MA: Blackwell, 2000).

negatively received by spectators, who decry the lack of respect for the original story or find the movie less engaging and pleasing than the novel. Less frequently, film adaptations are acclaimed by spectators and critics as superior to the novels or short stories that inspired them.

What most people tend to forget is that adaptations are not translations of the original works. Rather, an adaptation is always an interpretation. In the same way that two readers will never read the same novel, because their interpretation of the events, environments, and characters represented in the story will be different, an adaptation is necessarily a subjective reading of the original text. Moreover, adaptations are creative interpretations, because they produce new texts or semiotic representations (cinema, television, comic, videoclip, etc.) driven by their own artistic motivations and structural constraints.

The fact is that stories cannot be contained in any particular medium or restricted to any predetermined set of rules. Once they have been told, in whatever form or shape, and as long as people pay attention to them, they become part of our cultural makeup. People are free to read them and use them as they like, whether it is for their own private enjoyment, or to adapt, transform, and share them with others. These adaptations may try to be as faithful as possible to what the adapter thinks is the original intention of the author or the true meaning of the text. But they can also subvert those meanings through irony, humour, and commentary, like the memes that proliferate in the Internet era. At the end of the day, stories are not there to be revered and conserved in a state of purity. They constitute the fundamental means by which we humans give meaning to our world. And as such, they are always open to new interpretations.[16]

Summary

- Narrative is the semiotic representation of a sequence of events, meaningfully connected by time and cause. Literary narratives use written language to represent the connected sequence of events.

- There are many ways to classify literary narratives into different genres, according, for example, to the truthfulness of the events (fiction and nonfiction), to the way the story is told (prose and verse), to the length of the story (novel and short story), or to the content of the story (adventure, science-fiction, fantasy, romance, etc.).

---

16 Umberto Eco, *The Open Work* (Cambridge, MA: Harvard University Press, 1989).

- Prose fiction is narrative written without a metrical pattern that tells an imaginary or invented story. The most common genres of prose fiction in modern literature are novels and short stories. Novels tend to be much longer than short stories.
- The semiotic model of narrative, developed in the field of narratology, makes a key distinction between discourse (how the narrative is conveyed from the implied author to the implied reader) and story (what the narrator tells the narratee).
- Prose fictions are part of the manifold narratives that we humans use to communicate relevant meanings to each other through a wide variety of media, such as film, television, comics, etc.

References

Abbott, H. Porter, *The Cambridge Introduction to Narrative* (Cambridge, UK: Cambridge University Press, 2008), https://doi.org/10.1017/cbo9780511816932

Bal, Mieke, *Narratology: Introduction to the Theory of Narrative* (Toronto, CA: University of Toronto Press, 2017).

Barthes, Roland, 'Introduction to the Structural Analysis of Narrative,' in *A Roland Barthes Reader*, ed. by Susan Sontag, trans. by Stephen Heath (London, UK: Vintage, 1994), pp. 251–95.

Bascom, William, 'The Forms of Folklore: Prose Narratives,' *The Journal of American Folklore*, 78:307 (1965), 3–20.

Booth, Wayne C., *The Rhetoric of Fiction* (Chicago, IL: University of Chicago Press, 1983).

Buchanan, Daniel Crump, *One Hundred Famous Haiku* (Tokyo: Japan Publications, 1973).

Burroway, Janet, *Writing Fiction: A Guide to Narrative Craft* (Chicago, IL: University of Chicago Press, 2019), https://doi.org/10.7208/chicago/9780226616728.001.0001

Chatman, Seymour Benjamin, *Reading Narrative Fiction* (New York, NY: Macmillan, 1993).

Chatman, Seymour Benjamin, *Story and Discourse: Narrative Structure in Fiction and Film* (Ithaca, NY: Cornell University Press, 2000).

Cobley, Paul, *Narrative* (London, UK: Routledge, 2014).

Eco, Umberto, *The Open Work* (Cambridge, MA: Harvard University Press, 1989).

Herman, David, *Basic Elements of Narrative* (Chichester, UK: Wiley-Blackwell, 2009), https://doi.org/10.1002/9781444305920

Iser, Wolfgang, *The Implied Reader: Patterns of Communication in Prose Fiction from Bunyan to Beckett* (Baltimore, MD: Johns Hopkins University Press, 1995).

Johansen, Jørgen Dines, *Literary Discourse: A Semiotic-Pragmatic Approach to Literature* (Toronto: University of Toronto Press, 2002), https://doi.org/10.3138/9781442676725

Lodge, David, *The Art of Fiction: Illustrated from Classic and Modern Texts* (New York, NY: Viking, 1993).

Manguel, Alberto, *A History of Reading* (New York, NY: Penguin Books, 2014).

Onega Jaén, Susana, and José Angel García Landa, eds., *Narratology: An Introduction* (London, UK: Routledge, 1996), https://doi.org/10.4324/9781315843018

Stam, Robert, *Film Theory: An Introduction* (Malden, MA: Blackwell, 2000).

word cloud of terms including: events, plot, story, conflict, emplotment, protagonist, narrative, example, narrator, George, princess, resolution, reader, plots, some, one, time, arrangement, ends, suspense, structure, beginning, another, novel, world, experience, many, While, between, meaningful, rode, duration, other, order, ways, after, happened, middle, important, motivated, move, call, presented, see, modify, narratee, different, overcome, way, end, simply, point, event, model, life, same, fortune, previous, readers, rising, stage, Fig, more, action, only, through, lake, without, internal, Oedipus, whether, two, stories, need, sequence, characters, form, fiction, narrates, kind, beginnings, find, recognition, succession, Even, causal, often, all, meaning, adventures, telling, Aristotle, connections, surprise, character, dragon, climax

2. Plot

In the previous chapter, we defined narrative as the semiotic representation of a sequence of events, meaningfully connected by time and cause. But what precisely are events? And what constitutes a sequence of events? Does it matter whether the connecting thread that makes up that sequence is time or cause, or perhaps both? These are some of the essential questions that we will try to untangle in this chapter.

To be sure, they are not easy questions to answer. Narratology has struggled with them for some time and has come up with a range of terms and theories that sometimes bring more confusion than clarity. We will not delve here into the complexities of theory or the endless terminological discussions that have plagued the field.[1] But we do need to introduce the key conceptual distinction between story and plot, which has been key to achieve a better understanding of the structure and function of narratives.

The concept of plot dates all the way back to Aristotle (Fig. 2.1), who defined *mythos* as the arrangement or 'organisation of events' and argued that it was the most important element of storytelling.[2] At the beginning of the twentieth century, the Russian formalists recovered this concept and established a key distinction between the 'story' (*fabula*) and the 'plot' (*szujet*) of a narrative.[3] In the English language, the translation of these terms has created and continues to create a considerable amount of confusion, derived from the fact that 'story' is used at the same time as a generic term for narrative and as a technical term in narratology. For the purpose of this textbook, we will obviate these problems and simply integrate this important distinction into the semiotic model of narrative presented in the previous chapter.

---

1 See *Handbook of Narratology*, ed. by Peter Hühn (New York, NY: Walter de Gruyter, 2009), https://doi.org/10.1515/9783110316469
2 Aristotle, *Poetics*, trans. by Malcolm Heath (London, UK: Penguin Books, 1996), p. 11.
3 Viktor Borisovic Sklovskij, *Theory of Prose* (Elmwood Park, IL: Dalkey Archive Press, 1991).

© Ignasi Ribó, CC BY 4.0   https://doi.org/10.11647/OBP.0187.02

Fig. 2.1
Bust of Aristotle. Marble Roman copy after a Greek bronze original by Lysippos from 330 BC. Ludovisi Collection, photograph by Jastrow (2006), Public Domain, https://commons.wikimedia.org/wiki/File:Aristotle_Altemps_Inv8575.jpg

First, we will discuss more precisely the distinction between story and plot, clarifying what we understand by an 'event' and the different ways in which the events of a narrative can be connected. Then we will look at the mechanisms of emplotment, the specific operations that can be applied to a story when arranging it into a plot. By arranging events in a meaningful and coherent structure that has a beginning, a middle, and an end, these mechanisms can result in many kinds of plot. We will look at a few of these, which are quite common in prose fiction. Most of these plots are motivated by a conflict, which can be external or internal, and lead to some form of resolution. We will look at this 'story as war' analogy and present a five-stage general structure that can be found in many narrative plots. Finally, we will discuss two important mechanisms of emplotment at the micro level, suspense and surprise, which are often used by writers to engage readers and hook them to the narrative.

2.1 The Thread of Narrative

As we pointed out earlier, the story is the message that the narrator communicates to the narratee in a narrative. In this sense, it refers to a set of events happening in an alternative world, which we call the storyworld. We can define narrative events as changes of state occurring in the storyworld.[4] Such a world could be an accurate reflection of the lifeworld of the writer and his readers or an imaginary world that has never actually

---

4 David Herman, 'Events and Event-Types', in *Routledge Encyclopedia of Narrative Theory*, ed. by David Herman, Manfred Jahn, and Marie-Laure Ryan (London, UK: Routledge, 2005), pp. 151–52, https://doi.org/10.4324/9780203932896

existed. Whatever the truthfulness of this storyworld, the events of the story are supposed to have happened in it. These events can be actions undertaken by characters, but they can simply be situations, incidents, experiences, or things that happen to them or to their environment.

Let us imagine a simplified story to clarify these ideas. In this story, we only have five events: (1) George rode to the lake, (2) George slew the dragon, (3) George rescued the princess, (4) George and the princess rode away from the lake, and (5) George and the princess got married in the castle. We can display these events as marks in a horizontal arrow representing time (see Fig. 2.2).

Fig. 2.2 Diagram showing events interconnected by time only. By Ignasi Ribó, CC BY.

This is an arrangement of the events according to their succession in time. And this is what we call the story. Of course, the events in this story are also implicitly connected by cause (for example, event three is the consequence of event two). But our arrangement does not stress those connections. It simply reflects when the events happened in relation to each other (event two comes after event one, event three after event two, etc.).

It is unlikely, however, that the narrator will arrange the events of the story in such a simple fashion when telling it to the narratee. One thing the narrator could do, for example, is to stress the causal connections between the events: (1) George rode to the lake looking for the princess, (2) George slew the dragon in order to rescue the princess, (3) After killing the dragon, George rescued the princess, (4) George and the princess rode away from the lake to find safety in her castle, and (5) The princess married George to thank him for rescuing her from the dragon. We can display the causal connections with curved lines (see Fig. 2.3).

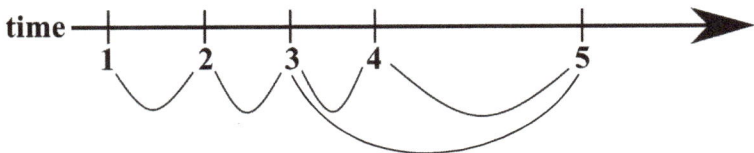

Fig. 2.3 Diagram showing events interconnected by time and cause. By Ignasi Ribó, CC BY.

Another thing that the narrator could do is to present the events in a different order, without necessarily following their sequence in time. For example, he could begin by telling the narratee about (1) the wedding between George and the princess, and only then go on to explain why the princess accepted George as her husband by telling how (2) George rode to the lake looking for the princess, (3) slew the dragon, and (4) escaped to safety with the princess. In this case, we would need to alter the representation of the sequence of events in the narrative (see Fig. 2.4).

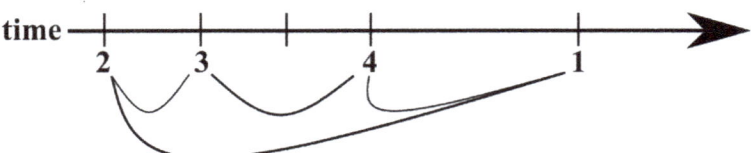

Fig. 2.4 Diagram showing events interconnected by time and cause, with the order of events altered by emplotment. By Ignasi Ribó, CC BY.

We call the actual arrangement of the sequence of events by the narrator of the story the 'plot.' Emplotment can involve simple modifications to the story, for example when the narrator tells the story 'as it happened.' But plots can also be much more complex and modify substantially the order of events, their duration, or the connections between them. As the novelist E. M. Forster explained,

> We have defined a story as a narrative of events arranged in their time-sequence. A plot is also a narrative of events, the emphasis falling on causality. 'The king died, and then the queen died,' is a story. 'The king died, and then the queen died of grief,' is a plot. The time-sequence is preserved, but the sense of causality overshadows it. Or again: 'The queen died, no one knew why, until it was discovered that it was through grief at the death of the king.' This is a plot with a mystery in it, a form capable of high development. It suspends the time-sequence, it moves as far away from the story as its limitations will allow. Consider the death of the queen. If it is in a story we say, 'and then?' If it is in a plot we ask, 'why?'[5]

2.2 Emplotment

Stories can be arranged into many kinds of plot. And there can never be a story without a plot, even if the plot is simply the presentation of events in their chronological succession, which would make the plot indistinguishable from the story. In fact, the story is only an abstraction, which is never accessed directly as such (either by the reader, the implied reader, or the narratee). What we read in a narrative is always a particular emplotment of the story.

For instance, the story of Saint George and the dragon, which we have simplified as an example in the previous section, has been told in different ways (Fig. 2.5). The succession of events is not the same in all these retellings. The narrator might begin the tale with the apparition of

---

5   E. M. Forster, *Aspects of the Novel* (San Diego, CA: Harcourt Brace Jovanovich, 1985), p. 86.

Fig. 2.5
Miniature of St. George and the Dragon, ms. of *Legenda aurea*, Paris (1382). British Library Royal 19 B XVII, f. 109, Public Domain, https://upload.wikimedia.org/wikipedia/commons/e/ef/St_George_Royal19BXVII_109.jpg

the plague-bearing dragon that poisons the lake and forces the kingdom to sacrifice their children to appease the beast. But the narrator might also begin with George riding near the lake and hearing the cries of distress from the princess. Some retellings invest much time recreating the conversation between George and the princess at that moment, while others move directly to the fight between George and the dragon. In some retellings of the story, George marries the princess at the end. But in others the marriage, whether it happened or not, is left out of the tale. All these versions stem from different decisions on the part of the authors and result in different plots of the same story. We call emplotment the process of arranging the events of the story into a narrative message communicated by the narrator to the narratee.

Emplotment involves five basic operations:[6]

1. *Order*: The sequence of events in the plot may or may not follow a strict chronological succession. Emplotment can modify the order in which the events are presented by the narrator, for example by beginning at some point in the middle of the story (*in medias res*) and then jumping back to events that happened earlier (flashback) or later (flashforward).

2. *Duration*: The duration of the events in the plot may or may not reflect the actual duration of those events in the story. Emplotment can modify the duration of the events presented by the narrator, for example by compressing time (e.g. telling fifty years in the life of a character in one paragraph) or expanding time (e.g. describing a kiss that lasted for one second in ten pages).

---

6 Based on Gérard Genette, *Narrative Discourse: An Essay in Method* (Ithaca, NY: Cornell University Press, 1990).

3. *Frequency*: The number of times that events are repeated in a plot may or may not reflect the number of times that those events occurred in the story. Emplotment can modify the frequency of the events presented by the narrator, for example by repeating the same event several times in the plot (repetition, e.g. telling the same murder from different perspectives) or collapsing several events of similar nature into a single event (iteration, e.g. telling the protagonist's daily work routine as one exemplary set of events happening on any given day).

4. *Connection*: The connections between the events in the plot may or may not reflect the actual connections between the events in the story. Emplotment can modify the meaning of the events presented by the narrator through the establishment of explicit or implicit causal connections between them. Ultimately, of course, it will depend on the reader's interpretation to determine which causal connections need to be retained from the narrative beyond the basic chronological succession of events.

5. *Relevance*: Similarly, the information about the events provided in the plot may or may not exhaust the actual information that is relevant about those events in the story. Emplotment can modify the meaning of the events presented by the narrator by providing or withholding information related to those events. Once again, the reader will have to interpret which of the pieces of information presented are relevant and fill in the gaps left by the narrator.

Not every plot applies all these operations to the story. As we have seen, it is even possible to have a plot that does not modify or add causality to the chronological succession of events. These operations are simply theoretical possibilities, which writers may or may not use to arrange the events of the story told by the narrator.

2.3 Beginnings, Middles, and Ends

As pointed out by Aristotle in his *Poetics*, plots are generally arranged to have a beginning, a middle, and an end.[7] But Aristotle was not simply stating the obvious fact that plots start at some point, extend during some time, and finish at another point. What he meant is that plots have an internal coherence that connects beginnings with endings through a meaningful and purposeful development. Unlike events in life, which simply happen, without any coherence or purpose, emplotted events are

---

7 Aristotle, pp. 13–14.

meaningfully connected to form a coherent whole. In real life, there is no such thing as a 'beginning' or an 'ending,' unless someone turns those events into a plot. Even a person's birth or death are unconnected events, without any meaning or significance in the general scheme of things. We need to emplot those two events, together with whatever happens in the middle, into some kind of narrative (e.g. 'he was born in 1903, worked as an accountant during most of his life, and died peacefully in his own bed aged 82') before they become a beginning and an end, the opening and closure of a biographical plot.

Biography, the narrative of a person's life, is a type of plot that seems quite natural to us, accustomed as we are to see ourselves and other individuals as coherent and meaningful entities. It is not surprising, therefore, that biographical plots have often been used by fiction writers to arrange their stories. For example, Daniel Defoe's classic novel *Robinson Crusoe* (Fig. 2.6) begins with the eponymous character's birth and goes on to narrate his life adventures, including the time he spent as a castaway on a remote desert island. Although the novel ends somewhere in the middle of Robinson's life, while promising a second part to the story, the organising principle of the plot is clearly biographical.

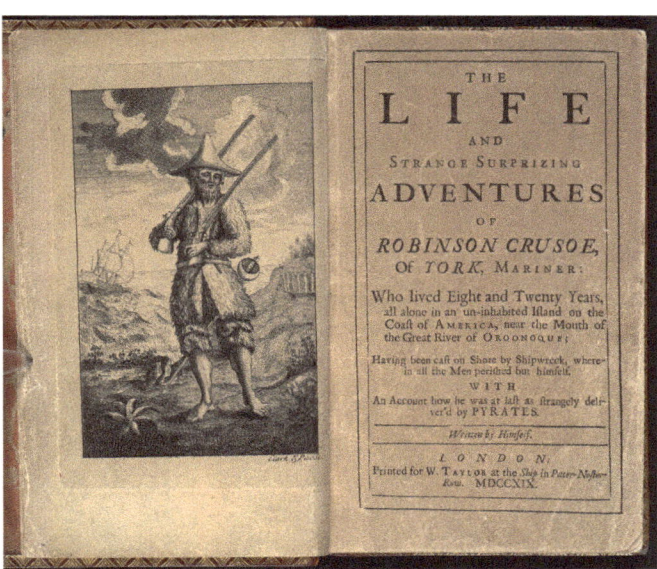

Fig. 2.6 Title page and portrait of Robinson Crusoe in the first edition of Daniel Defoe's *The Life and Strange Surprizing Adventures of Robinson Crosoe* (1719). British Library, Ambre Troizat, CC BY-SA 4.0, https://upload.wikimedia.org/wikipedia/commons/f/f1/The_life_and_Strange_Surprizing_Adventures_of_Robinson_Crosoe%2C_London%2C_1719.png

But biography is only one of the many kinds of plot that we find in narrative. Since Aristotle, many typologies of plot (sometimes called masterplots)

have been proposed.[8] While the best of these typologies might be able to capture certain recurrent aspects of emplotment, they can never embrace all possible narrative plots. Provided we take these typologies as an orientation, and avoid turning them into rigid and normative taxonomies, they can help us to better understand the various ways in which narrators can arrange the events of the plot.

For example, the following are seven kinds of plot that we often find in popular novels and short stories, described in terms of beginnings, middles, and ends:[9]

Fig. 2.7
Illustration of 'Hansel and Gretel' by Arthur Rackham (1909), Public Domain, https://upload.wikimedia.org/wikipedia/commons/d/d1/Hansel-and-gretel-rackham.jpg

1. *Overcoming the monster*: It begins with the protagonist setting out to defeat an evil (or threatening) force; it narrates the fight between the hero and this monster; and it ends with the defeat of the monster. For example, in 'Hansel and Gretel' (Fig. 2.7), a German fairy tale recorded by the Brothers Grimm, two children try to escape from the forest house of a witch who has kidnapped them and intends to eat them.

---

8   See Seymour Benjamin Chatman, *Story and Discourse: Narrative Structure in Fiction and Film* (Ithaca, NY: Cornell University Press, 2000).
9   Christopher Booker, *The Seven Basic Plots: Why We Tell Stories* (London: Continuum, 2004).

2. *From rags to riches*: It begins with a poor protagonist; it narrates how she goes on to acquire wealth and power, but then loses everything again (or loses and regains it once more); and it ends with her becoming wiser thanks to the experience. An example of this kind of plot is the Middle Eastern folk tale 'Aladdin and the Magic Lamp,' often included in *One Thousand and One Nights*, which tells the adventures of a young and poor orphan who becomes rich and powerful with the help of a genie.

3. *The quest*: It begins with the protagonist (and maybe some companions) setting out to obtain an important object; it narrates the many obstacles that they must face; and it ends with the successful completion of the quest. J. R. R. Tolkien's novel *The Hobbit* is a famous example of this kind of plot, where the hobbit Bilbo and his companions set out on a dangerous quest to recover the treasure guarded by a dragon.

4. *Voyage and return*: It begins with the protagonist departing her home for a strange land; it narrates the threats and adventures that she needs to overcome; and it ends with her return home enriched by the experience. Lewis Carroll's fantasy novel *Alice's Adventures in Wonderland*, where the protagonist suddenly finds herself in a strange underground world, is a well-known example of this kind of plot.

5. *Comedy*: It begins with a light and humorous protagonist; it narrates the various circumstances and problems that she must overcome; and it ends with the happy resolution of these circumstances or problems. An example of a novel with this kind of plot is Jane Austen's *Sense and Sensibility*, where the Dashwood sisters end up happily married after all sorts of complications.

6. *Tragedy*: It begins with a protagonist who is affected by some sort of mistake or flaw that is the origin of a certain conflict; it narrates how he tries to overcome this conflict; and it ends with his failure to do so, and perhaps with the recognition of his mistake or flaw. A modern example of this kind of plot is Vladimir Nabokov's controversial novel *Lolita*, where the sexual obsession of an aged literature professor for a twelve-year-old girl leads him to commit successive transgressions until he dies in prison.

7. *Rebirth*: It begins with the protagonist living her normal life; it narrates how certain circumstances (normally adverse ones) force her to change her life; and it ends with her transformation into a new person capable of overcoming those circumstances. A well-known example of this kind of plot is Charles Dickens'

A Christmas Carol, where old Scrooge, a miser who is unable to partake in Christmas celebrations, becomes a kinder person after receiving the visit of several ghosts.

2.4 Conflict and Resolution

In the masterplots described above, the main characters (or protagonists) are motivated to act by some conflict. Whether this conflict is external (e.g. a monster or a circumstance that poses a threat) or internal (e.g. a mistake or a flaw in one's character), the kernel of the plot seems to be the need to overcome this conflict and find some form of resolution.

Ancient Greeks referred to conflict as *agon*. The importance of this concept for narrative can be grasped by the fact that we still call the leading character of a story its 'protagonist' (meaning, one who fights for something or someone). We also call the main enemy of this character, whether it is another character or some natural or supernatural force, the 'antagonist' (meaning, one who fights against something or someone).

Fig. 2.8
Oedipus and the Sphinx. Tondo of an Attic red-figure kylix, 480–470 BC. From Vulci. Photograph by Juan José Moral (2009), captured at Museo Gregoriano Etrusco, room XI, Public Domain, https://commons.wikimedia.org/wiki/File:Oidipous_sphinx_MGEt_16541_reconstitution.svg

In the *Poetics*, Aristotle claims that plots can be divided into those where the protagonist succeeds in overcoming the conflict (goes from misfortune to fortune, as in comedy) and those where the protagonist falls victim to the conflict (goes from fortune to misfortune, as in tragedy).[10] In both cases, there is a reversal of fortune (*peripeteia*) and some form of resolution, which may or may not involve a recognition or gain in knowledge for the protagonist (*anagnorisis*).[11] For example, in Sophocles' *Oedipus Rex* (Fig. 2.8), King Oedipus faces a devastating plague in his city of Thebes

---

10   Aristotle, pp. 8–9.
11   Aristotle, pp. 18–19.

(conflict) and seeks to find the person responsible for spreading the infection. A carefully crafted series of events lead Oedipus to discover (reversal of fortune and recognition) that the culprit is none other than himself, having unknowingly killed his father and married his own mother many years earlier. At the end, after his mother/wife commits suicide, Oedipus blinds himself and is banished from Thebes.

Aristotle's description of tragic conflict and resolution, as exemplified in *Oedipus Rex*, has been tremendously influential throughout history and has resulted in the view that all plots are essentially motivated by a conflict and move forward to close or resolve this conflict. This idea has been formalised in the five stages of Freytag's pyramid (Fig. 2.9), which was originally conceived to describe the conventional emplotment of dramatic plays in five acts,[12] but is often applied to narrative plots as well:

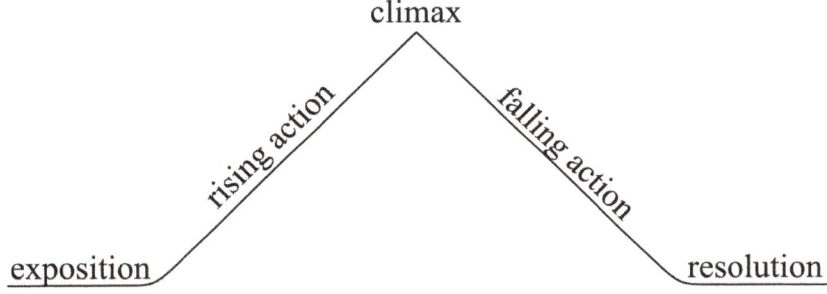

Fig. 2.9 Schema of Freytag's pyramid. By Ignasi Ribó, based on Gustav Freytag, *Freytag's Technique of the Drama: An Exposition of Dramatic Composition and Art*, trans. by Elias J MacEvan (Charleston, SC: Bibliobazaar, 2009), CC BY.

1. *Exposition*: In this initial stage, the environments and the characters, particularly the protagonist, are introduced. There is no conflict yet, but we might get indications about the conflicting goals of the characters and the motives that will drive the plot.

2. *Rising action*: At some point, the (external or internal) conflict is revealed and provokes a series of events (confrontations, reversals, adventures, etc.) that move the plot forward and always towards a higher degree of intensity. In novels and short stories, this stage tends to be the longest and includes most of the vicissitudes of the plot.

3. *Climax*: This is the point where the rising action achieves its maximum level of intensity and the conflict reaches the decisive confrontation. It is also a turning point, because from here on the conflict can only move towards the final resolution. The

---

12 Gustav Freytag, *Freytag's Technique of the Drama: An Exposition of Dramatic Composition and Art*, trans. by Elias J MacEvan (Charleston, SC: Bibliobazaar, 2009).

climax is not always an external event, such as a battle between the protagonist and the antagonist. It can also be a more subtle reversal of fortune, for example the recognition of one's own guilt, which decides the outcome of the conflict.

4. *Falling action*: The events that follow the climax might still be motivated by the conflict, but they tend to wane in intensity and progressively lead to some form of resolution. Characters settle their confrontations, solve or abandon their problems, overcome or submit to existing threats and enemies. In one way or another, the climax has already decided the outcome of the conflict and the falling action needs to bring the situation back to an equilibrium. In prose fiction, this stage is often much shorter and does not include as many events as the rising action.

5. *Resolution*: At the end, the conflict has been solved, either because the protagonist or the antagonist have won, or because they have found some way to solve their disagreements, or simply because they have exhausted their capacity to continue fighting. In the resolution stage, we might be shown what the characters do after everything is settled or find answers for the outstanding questions. In prose fiction, this stage often tries to provide a sense of closure.

This model, based on a 'story as war' analogy, is often presented as the only way to emplot a story. While it is true that many popular fiction stories follow this pattern in one way or another, there are other plots, particularly in modern and contemporary literature, that depart quite significantly from the dynamic of conflict and resolution that author Ursula K. Le Guin described as the 'gladiatorial view of fiction':

> People are cross-grained, aggressive, and full of trouble, the storytellers tell us; people fight themselves and one another, and their stories are full of their struggles. But to say that that is the story is to use one aspect of existence, conflict, to subsume all other aspects, many of which it does not include and does not comprehend.[13]

While perhaps not as common, there are alternative models of emplotment that reflect these other aspects of existence. One such model could be 'story as birth,' where the plot is motivated, not by conflict, but by the desire and the struggle to arise and grow, as in the experience of many living things.[14] A novel that seems to follow this model of plot is Virginia Woolf's *To The*

---

13 Quoted in Janet Burroway, *Writing Fiction: A Guide to Narrative Craft* (Chicago, IL: University of Chicago Press, 2019), p. 133, https://doi.org/10.7208/chicago/9780226616728.001.0001

14 Burroway, p. 134.

Lighthouse. While this story does not lack elements of conflict or tension, its plot is mainly arranged by the emergence of emotions in the subjective experience of the characters, for example through the creative process that Lily Briscoe undergoes before she is able to complete her painting at the end of the novel.

Yet another model, somehow related to the organic analogy of the previous one, but also incorporating Aristotle's theory of recognition (*anagnorisis*)[15] and James Joyce's conception of epiphany,[16] is 'story as illumination,' where the protagonist moves from darkness to light, from ignorance to knowledge, without the need to engage in any form of conflict. In Joyce's collection of short stories, *Dubliners*, for example, characters experience sudden moments of illumination (epiphany) that give them a new understanding of their world and produce a meaningful change in their lives.

Even when modern prose fiction follows the war analogy and uses conflict to motivate the plot, it often presents these conflicts as fundamentally unresolvable. Many authors see the classic idea of an ending that brings resolution to the conflict as unrealistic and only fit for entertainment. Thus, open and ambiguous endings are quite common in serious modern literature, which tends to avoid providing the reader with an artificial sense of closure ('and they lived happily ever after'). Even in these narratives, however, there is often some form of ending. While they might leave many questions unanswered at the end, it is precisely this questioning that provides meaning and gives coherence to the whole plot.

2.5 Suspense and Surprise

So far, we have been speaking of plots at a macro level. But there are two important mechanisms of emplotment, suspense and surprise, which operate at the micro level, particularly as the events move through the rising action towards the climax of the plot (provided that the plot follows Freytag's pyramid or a similar structure). These mechanisms cross over in some ways from story to discourse, but we need to discuss them here to complete our presentation of plot.

Suspense is a phenomenon that derives from the arrangement of events in the plot, but which cannot exist without the reader. It arises from the gap between what the reader knows from the previous events in the plot and what she anticipates is going to happen next.[17] In a way, it

---

15 Aristotle, pp. 18–19.
16 Irene Hendry, 'Joyce's Epiphanies,' *The Sewanee Review,* 54:3 (1946), 449–67.
17 Teresa Bridgeman, 'Time and Space,' in *The Cambridge Companion to Narrative,* ed. by David Herman (Cambridge, UK: Cambridge University Press, 2007), pp. 52–65, https://doi.org/10.1017/ccol0521856965

stems from the curiosity of the reader asking herself 'and then what?' as the plot unfolds.

Suspense can be heightened when the reader knows more than the characters, or even the narrator. For example, the reader might know that the killer is hiding in the bedroom of the detective's girlfriend, as he walks unwittingly back home after leaving her at the door of her apartment.

But suspense can be created simply by arranging the events in the plot in a way that ignites the curiosity of the reader. For example, the reader, as well as the detective and his girlfriend, might know that there is a killer on the loose. Certain events in the plot might indicate that the killer is moving on to murder the detective's girlfriend (a cigarette butt found in her apartment, a strange midnight call, etc.). The anticipation of future events through hints given earlier in the plot is called foreshadowing. Using foreshadowing is generally enough to create suspense, and it is a common technique in some genres, such as mystery and horror fiction. When the event foreshadowed never actually happens, it is called a red herring, a technique that is sometimes employed to mislead and surprise readers.

While suspense depends on the reader's knowledge (or suspicion) of events to come, surprise is an effect of the reader's ignorance.[18] As the plot unfolds, the reader anticipates future events based on what she already knows. If something unexpected happens, that is a surprise. When they affect crucial kernels in the plot or alter the situation of the main characters, surprises are the kind of twists that make readers gasp and experience the thrill of unforeseen revelation. For example, if the reader suddenly discovers that the killer is actually the detective's girlfriend, who has been preparing her alibi before moving on to murder the detective, the whole plot takes a surprising new direction.

Suspense and surprise can work together in the plot to great effect. By keeping the reader always alert, not knowing whether the next event will be the confirmation of a suspenseful anticipation or an unexpected twist, emplotment can create the kind of narrative tension that hooks readers to the book and compels them to keep turning the pages.

Summary

- Story is the arrangement of events according to their sequence in time, while plot is the arrangement of the events by the narrator when telling them to the narratee. In addition to the temporal connection, events in the plot generally have a causal connection.

---

18   Seymour Benjamin Chatman, *Reading Narrative Fiction* (New York, NY: Macmillan, 1993), p. 21.

- Emplotment is the arrangement of the events of the story by modifying their order, duration, frequency, connection, or relevance, in order to make a plot.

- Plots have an internal coherence that connects beginnings with ends through a meaningful and purposeful development.

- While there are various ways to connect beginnings with ends, emplotment is often motivated by a fundamental conflict or tension that moves the plot through the stages of exposition, rising action, climax, falling action, and resolution.

- Emplotment can engage the reader by creating anticipation about future events through suspense and foreshadowing, while at the same time disproving the reader's expectations through surprise.

References

Aristotle, *Poetics*, trans. by Malcolm Heath (London, UK: Penguin Books, 1996).

Booker, Christopher, *The Seven Basic Plots: Why We Tell Stories* (London, UK: Continuum, 2004).

Bridgeman, Teresa, 'Time and Space,' in *The Cambridge Companion to Narrative*, ed. by David Herman (Cambridge, UK: Cambridge University Press, 2007), pp. 52–65, https://doi.org/10.1017/ccol0521856965

Burroway, Janet, *Writing Fiction: A Guide to Narrative Craft* (Chicago, IL: University of Chicago Press, 2019), https://doi.org/10.7208/chicago/9780226616728.001.0001

Chatman, Seymour Benjamin, *Reading Narrative Fiction* (New York, NY: Macmillan, 1993).

Chatman, Seymour Benjamin, *Story and Discourse: Narrative Structure in Fiction and Film* (Ithaca, NY: Cornell University Press, 2000).

Forster, E. M., *Aspects of the Novel* (San Diego, CA: Harcourt Brace Jovanovich, 1985).

Freytag, Gustav, *Freytag's Technique of the Drama: An Exposition of Dramatic Composition and Art*, trans. by Elias J MacEvan (Charleston, SC: Bibliobazaar, 2009).

Genette, Gérard, *Narrative Discourse: An Essay in Method* (Ithaca, NY: Cornell University Press, 1990).

Hendry, Irene, 'Joyce's Epiphanies,' *The Sewanee Review*, 54:3 (1946), 449–67.

Herman, David, 'Events and Event-Types,' in *Routledge Encyclopedia of Narrative Theory*, ed. by David Herman, Manfred Jahn, and Marie-Laure Ryan (London, UK: Routledge, 2005), pp. 151–52, https://doi.org/10.4324/9780203932896

Hühn, Peter, ed., *Handbook of Narratology* (New York, NY: Walter de Gruyter, 2009), https://doi.org/10.1515/9783110316469

Sklovskij, Viktor Borisovic, *Theory of Prose* (Elmwood Park, IL: Dalkey Archive Press, 1991).

relationships
environment
meaningful
narrative
call
fiction
atmosphere
other
like
literary
setting
time
any
own
Fig
spatial
Domain
mental
Harry
create
elements
kind
temporal
more
things
existents
space
represented
place
one
while
stage
between
novels
reader
particular
many
arranged
about
atmospheric
rather
make
all
narrator
experience
environments
only
imagination
description
real
stories
less
nonfiction
readers
way
house
used
words
just
natural
storyworld
often
chapter
being
verisimilitude
short
arrangement
seem
significant
world
objects
prose
include
development
character
novel
artificial
mind
distinction
some
narratives
descriptions
represent
events
plot
true
story
barometer
discourse
different
details
topography
recreate
through
take
found
characterisation
example

3. Setting

As we have seen, the temporal dimension is represented in narrative by the plot, which is an arrangement of the events in the story. But what about the spatial dimension? How are the environments where these events take place arranged in narrative? What aspects of those environments are communicated to the narratee by the narrator? What is the relationship of narrative environments with the other existents of the story, characters and events? And how are literary narratives able to induce mental images of those environments in their readers using only words? These are some of the questions that we will try to answer in this chapter.

If plot is the meaningful arrangement of the events (temporal existents) of the story, setting can be conceived as the meaningful arrangement of the story's environments (spatial existents). An existent in this context is simply something that exists, i.e. that is the case or has being, in a particular world. In our semiotic model of narrative, we distinguish three types of existents in any given storyworld: events, environments, and characters (Fig. 3.1).

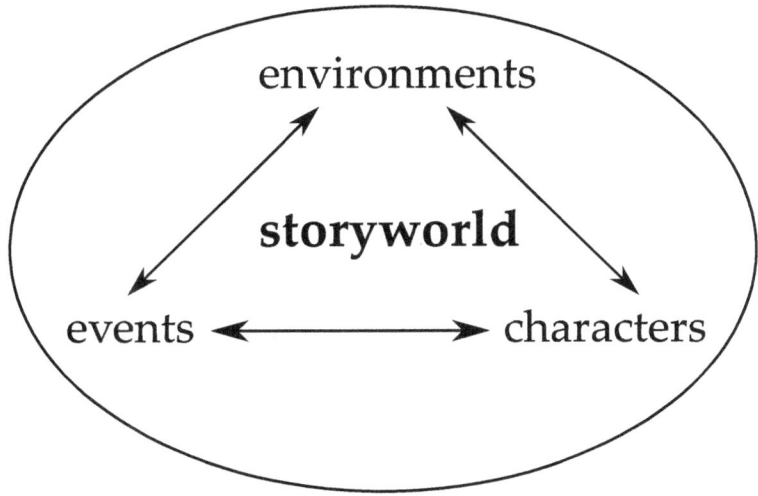

Fig. 3.1 Relationships between existents in the storyworld. By Ignasi Ribó, CC BY.

© Ignasi Ribó, CC BY 4.0   https://doi.org/10.11647/OBP.0187.03

In reality, however, things are not so simple. Rather than being two separate entities, space and time are intimately connected in what physicists call space-time continuum and literary theorists refer to as the chronotope.[1] In English, we say that 'events take place,' reflecting the realisation that events can never happen separated from space, or rather from a particular place. In fact, the distinction between space and time is only an abstraction, an attempt to untangle and better understand the complex processes that make up our own lifeworld. Similarly, the distinction between environments (space) and events (time) in the storyworld should be taken as an abstraction to help us to understand the structure of narrative. Actually, both are intimately related and often intersect in complex ways.

And it is not just environments and events that are interconnected. In the previous chapter, when analysing the process of emplotment, we have seen some of the close connections that link events with characters. Similarly, environments and characters are also intimately connected with each other. Environments are more than just an objective background, or a stage filled with things (landscapes, buildings, furniture, etc.) where characters act. At a fundamental level, environments are the meaningful entanglements of characters with their own world, often represented in narrative as the subjective or psychological aspect of setting.

In this chapter, we will discuss in some detail how the environments of the storyworld are arranged in narrative. We will begin by defining what we understand by environment and the crucial role of environments in building the world of short stories and novels. We will then distinguish two basic ways to arrange environments into a fictional setting: as a topographical layout of natural and artificial things in space or as atmospheric relationships between those same things and the characters of the story. This distinction will allow us to present a typology with four major kinds of setting that may be found in prose fiction: irrelevant, functional, mental, and symbolic. We will then see how literary narratives use description to represent the setting and induce in the reader's mind a vivid image of the storyworld. Finally, we will discuss the notion of verisimilitude and show how literary description can be used to encourage readers to read fictional stories as if they were happening in the 'real' world.

3.1 The World of Narrative

All narratives involve the creation of a particular world, the world of the story or storyworld, with its own temporal and spatial existents.[2] Most

---

1 Mikhail M. Bakhtin, *The Dialogic Imagination: Four Essays*, trans. by Michael Holquist and Caryl Emerson (Austin, TX: University of Texas Press, 2011).
2 See David Herman, *Basic Elements of Narrative* (Chichester, UK: Wiley-Blackwell, 2009), https://doi.org/10.1002/9781444305920

often, this world is very similar to our own lifeworld. Things appear and behave just as they do in our everyday experience. When a character throws a pebble into a pond, the pebble bounces a few times and then sinks in the water. This is what we call realism, a principle of narrative discourse that uses our perceptions and assumptions about our lifeworld, which is often described as the 'real world,' to build, with more or less accuracy, the world of the story.

But the world created by narrative discourse can also be very different from our own. In a science-fiction short story, for example, the pebble that the character throws into the pond might rebound and fly out to space. Storyworlds are not necessarily bound by the same physical laws that seem to rule our world. They are alternative or possible worlds, configurations of space and time that may defy any aspect of common sense or our everyday experience.[3] Fiction genres like fantasy, horror, or science fiction make much use of this worldbuilding capacity of narrative. But more realistic genres, such as romance, thriller, or comedy, even nonfiction books, also create their own storyworlds through the arrangement of the different existents of the story.

In most narratives, environments tend to be the existents of the story that contribute more directly to worldbuilding. An environment is everything that surrounds the characters, including landscapes, trees, animals, buildings, rooms, furniture, and any other natural or man-made objects or structures that characters may inhabit or move through.

Some stories take place in a single environment. This environment might be quite limited in scope, like the room where the protagonist of Franz Kafka's *The Metamorphosis* becomes trapped after turning into a giant insect (Fig. 3.2). But single environments can also be quite extensive and include various spaces, like the different chambers, corridors, and dungeons at Hogwarts castle in the Harry Potter novels.

Many novels take place in a variety of environments, where the different characters evolve and interact. For example, in Leo Tolstoy's *War and Peace*, a vast chronicle of the Napoleonic wars in Russia, there are two main environments where the story unfolds, Moscow and Saint Petersburg. But other environments are also important for the novel's plot, such as the locations of crucial battles like Austerlitz, Smolensk, or Borodino.

There are also short stories and novels, particularly in the genres of adventure and travel narrative, where the movement through different environments is the fundamental driver of the plot. In Jules Verne's *Around the World in Eighty Days*, for example, Phileas Fogg travels from London to Suez, Bombay, Calcutta, Hong Kong, Yokohama, San Francisco,

---

3 Marie-Laure Ryan, *Possible Worlds, Artificial Intelligence, and Narrative Theory* (Bloomington, IN: Indiana University Press, 1991).

Fig. 3.2
Cover of an early German edition of Franz Kafka's *The Metamorphosis* (*Die Verwandlung*, 1915), Public Domain, https://commons.wikimedia.org/wiki/Category:Kafka_Die_Verwandlung#/media/File:Kafka_Verwandlung_016.jpg

New York, and back to London, in a hectic and adventure-filled journey motivated by a wager.

Whichever environments make up the storyworld, whether it is a lonely house in the hills or a multiverse with many different galaxies, prose fiction needs to arrange and represent those environments in one way or another. This is what we call the setting of the story, which might comprise an arrangement of objects and landmarks in space (topography) or a more subjective experience of place (atmosphere).

3.2 Topography and Atmosphere

Environments can be represented topographically, as an arrangement of natural and artificial objects or things laid out in space. Natural things can include clouds, mountains, paths, trees, plants, flowers, rocks, rivers, animals, and so on. They can also include people when they are not characters, but simply background elements of the story. Artificial things can include buildings, walls, doors, windows, furniture, machines, tools, and many other man-made objects and structures. What matters in a topography is the quality of all these things and the spatial relationships between them, which define the particular features of a given landscape or interior.

Topographies often serve as mere backgrounds for the actions and interactions of the characters, very much like a theatre stage where events happen and characters speak to each other. This stage can be more or less elaborate, more or less naturalistic, but it is arranged and represented as if it could stand on its own, once all the characters have left and there are no more events to tell. Topographic setting is thus related to a certain cultural conception of our own existence, one that sees humans as self-reliant individuals (or embodied souls) acting out their temporal lives in the vast stage that is the objective world.

While topographical setting is very common in film and drama, it is less common in literary narrative, at least in a pure form. An objective description of objects and spatial relationships might help the reader to create in her mind a visual representation of the story's environment, but the true interest of the story lies in the way characters experience their own environment.

We call atmosphere the arrangement or representation of natural and artificial things, not as they stand on their own, but in their association with characters' actions, thoughts, feelings, and experiences. The distinction between topography and atmosphere parallels the distinction in geography between 'space,' the abstract and undifferentiated extension of location, and 'place,' which emerges when human beings give meaning to that location, both by experiencing it and conceptualising it in language.[4]

In narrative, atmosphere can be represented through the emotions that a certain environment induces in one or more of the characters of the story. For example, in J. R. R. Tolkien's fantasy trilogy *The Lord of the Rings*, the atmosphere of the Shire, an idyllic countryside with meadows and little farmhouses, where Frodo and the other hobbits live, is very different from their destination, the barren and ominous Mordor, the dark land of Sauron (Fig. 3.3). As Frodo and his friends approach Mordor, the narrator often highlights the contrast between these environments through the feelings of fear, desolation, and even insanity that grip the characters and tint the different environments with an increasingly oppressive atmosphere.

Atmosphere can also be represented by the tone of the narrative. The narrator's choice of language, as he describes the different environments in the story, can create various atmospheric effects. Tone is generally an aspect of narrative discourse, but it can also be an element of the story, particularly when it reflects the emotions or subjective perceptions of characters. In Charles Dickens' *Great Expectations*, for example, the tone used by Pip, the narrator and protagonist, changes throughout the novel, providing atmospheric descriptions of the different environments

---

4 Yi-Fu Tuan, *Space and Place: The Perspective of Experience* (Minneapolis, MN: University of Minnesota Press, 2011).

Fig. 3.3 Map of Middle Earth, the fantasy world of J. R. R. Tolkien's novels. CC BY-SA 4.0, https://commons.wikimedia.org/wiki/File:World_map_.jpg

he experiences, such as the gloomy Kent countryside, the mysterious marshes, the dazzling city of London, or the gothic ruins of Satis House.

In some stories, atmosphere does not stem from the subjectivity of any character but is rather a projection of dominant social and cultural values. In Jane Austen's *Pride and Prejudice*, for example, environments like castles, country houses, and elegant sitting rooms are tinted by the cultural conventions and expectations of the English upper classes, whose wealth and social position allowed them to enjoy a privileged, if not always happy, lifestyle. In contrast, the environments of some of Émile Zola's novels are marked by the miserable day-to-day existence of the lower classes in France, like the shafts, railways, and shacks where miners dwell in *Germinal* (Fig. 3.4). When we discuss theme, we will see that the contrast between different social atmospheres in the same narrative can be a powerful instrument to criticise social arrangements, as in the vast panorama of nineteenth century French society depicted in Honoré de Balzac's sequence of novels *The Human Comedy*.

3.3 Kinds of Setting

Not surprisingly, we tend to find a great variety of settings in prose fiction. There is an almost inexhaustible number of environments where the events of a plot can take place. And those environments can be arranged in many ways, notably by making different decisions regarding topographic and atmospheric description.

Fig. 3.4 Pit No. 10 of the Compagnie des mines de Béthune, Nord-Pas-de-Calais, France (ca. 1910), Public Domain, https://commons.wikimedia.org/wiki/File:Sains-en-Gohelle_-_Fosse_n%C2%B0_10_-_10_bis_des_mines_de_B%C3%A9thune_(B).jpg

Such diversity has prevented narratological theory from coming up with typologies of setting like the ones that have been proposed for plot or characterisation. Below, we present a classification of setting based on the relative importance of topography and atmosphere, as well as on the connections between the environments and the other existents of the story, events and characters. Once again, this typology should only be taken as an orientation. There are many stories whose setting does not fall squarely into any of these categories. And the environments of many others are arranged by combining different kinds of setting.

1. *Irrelevant*: Setting does not matter much for the story. The narrator provides minimal or no information about topography or atmosphere, and the characters do not seem particularly conscious or affected by setting in any way. Rather, they seem to move through a neutral and featureless space. They might even behave as disembodied minds. Irrelevant setting is quite rare in prose fiction, but it is a possibility. One example of this kind of setting can be found in Samuel Beckett's existentialist novel *The Unnamable*.

2. *Functional*: Setting is presented in order to support the development of characters or the unfolding of events. The narrator provides only the information needed to sustain the story. Descriptions tend to emphasise topography rather than atmosphere. But atmospheric description can also be used when it serves to support plot or characterisation. Popular novels often

use this kind of setting, laying out space as a multidimensional stage for the development of the plot. One example is Dan Brown's bestseller *The Da Vinci Code*.

3. *Mental*: Setting is presented from the perspective of one of the characters, as a kind of inner experience or landscape of the mind. Most descriptions are heavily atmospheric, but topography might also be used occasionally. Setting and characterisation are closely integrated. This is the kind of setting that is often used in dramatic and psychological fiction to highlight the inner life of the main character and heighten the identification of the reader. An example of this kind of setting can be found in Virginia Woolf's modernist novel *Mrs Dalloway*.

4. *Symbolic*: Setting is presented in order to call attention or give prominence to other elements of story or discourse, by establishing a meaningful relationship between these elements and a particular environment. Symbolic setting might be related with plot (e.g. foreshadowing future events), characterisation (e.g. reflecting or contrasting the personality of characters), or theme (e.g. representing abstract ideas). Edgar Allan Poe's gothic horror story 'The Fall of the House of Usher' provides an example of this kind of setting.

3.4 Description

Unlike movies, literary narratives cannot represent setting directly. As the story is conveyed exclusively through words, there can be no visual or iconic representation of the environments where the story takes place. It rests on readers to recreate in their own imagination those environments based on the descriptions found in the text. Thus, every reader of Harry Potter's novels will imagine Hogwarts in their own particular way (Fig. 3.5). This is not the case for spectators of the film adaptations, all of whom see on the screen the exact same setting, a visual recreation of the literary environment based on the interpretative and framing decisions made by the movie's director and crew.

In general, a description is a text that represents environments or characters. Narrators in prose fiction may provide only a minimal description of the environment, sometimes nothing more than an indication: 'The detective arrived home and found his girlfriend pointing a gun at him.' But narrators can also represent the environment with all sorts of particular and sensory details: 'The house was dark and cold. Fumbling for the light switch, the detective saw that the window of his bedroom was wide open. He did not remember having left it open. The

Fig. 3.5
Hogwarts Castle in the ride *Harry Potter and the Forbidden Journey* at The Wizarding World of Harry Potter, Universal Studios Islands of Adventure Orlando, Florida. Source: Marcos Becerra, CC BY 2.0, https://www.flickr.com/photos/mbecerra/6402825573

curtains flapped against the pale moonlight. The rain had soaked the carpet and left a dark stain on the bed sheets. He heard a familiar voice whispering from the deepest corner of the room. The light blinked and he saw the gun pointing at him.'

Detailed descriptions of the environment are not always appreciated by readers or critics. Some argue that they are too static and halt the flow of the plot or the development of character, which are supposed to be the fundamental components of the story. Thus, inexperienced writers are often encouraged to avoid lengthy descriptions and to make them as 'narrative' as possible. But descriptions are already narrative. They allow environments, which are basic existents of the story, to be represented. In this way, they contribute to the recreation of the storyworld in the imagination of the reader.

Descriptions can be sharp and quick, using only as many words as needed to fix the setting in the mind of the reader while letting the characters and events move forward, as in Ernest Hemingway's short stories and novels. But they can also be long, meticulous and intricate like a tapestry (see Fig. 3.6), as in Marcel Proust's seven-volume novel *In Search of Lost Time*, where environments, more than being mere background, become as relevant for the story as the characters or the plot, if not more.

Whether it is long or short, an effective description usually requires the presentation of significant details about the environment being

Fig. 3.6
The Art of Painting (1666–1668), oil on canvas by Jan Vermeer, Public Domain, https://commons.wikimedia.org/wiki/File:Jan_Vermeer_-_The_Art_of_Painting_-_Google_Art_Project.jpg

described. A detail may be significant for different reasons. For example, details are significant when they reveal the character's emotional or perceptive connection with the environment. Or they can be significant for the development of the plot, by revealing the connection between the environment and the events of the story. Details can also be significant for the reader. In this sense, a crucial aim of narrative discourse is to allow readers to recreate the setting of the story in their imagination by providing them with vivid, concrete, and specific details about the story's environments.

> If those who have studied the art of writing are in accord on any one point, it is on this: the surest way to arouse and hold the attention of the reader is by being specific, definite and concrete. The greatest writers — Homer, Dante, Shakespeare — are effective largely because they deal in particulars and report the details that matter. Their words call up pictures.[5]

3.5 Verisimilitude

Apart from significant details that connect the different existents of the story and help the reader to imagine the setting, descriptions in prose fiction are often filled with insignificant or 'useless details.'[6] For example,

---

5   William Strunk and E. B. White, *The Elements of Style* (Boston, MA: Allyn and Bacon, 1999), pp. 30–31.
6   Roland Barthes, *The Rustle of Language* (Berkeley, CA: University of California Press, 1989), p. 142.

in Gustave Flaubert's short story 'A Simple Heart,' the narrator describes Madame Aubain's house as having, amongst other things, an old piano and a barometer (Fig. 3.7). While the piano might be there to recreate the atmosphere of a typical bourgeois home, the function of the barometer is less clear. It does not seem to be a necessary element of the environment and does not play any role in characterisation or emplotment. So, what is it doing there?

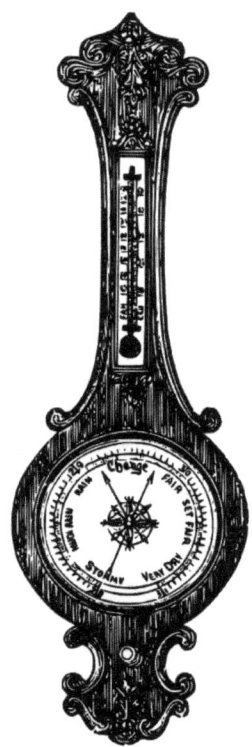

Fig. 3.7
Drawing of a wall barometer, Public Domain, https://pixabay.com/p-1297523

In his letters, the playwright Anton Chekhov famously recommended aspiring writers to 'remove everything that has no relevance to the story. If you say in the first chapter that there is a rifle hanging on the wall, in the second or third chapter it absolutely must go off. If it is not going to be fired, it should not be hanging there.'[7] This dramatic principle, known as 'Chekhov's gun,' stresses the functional role of setting, and in particular the necessary connection with the plot, through symbolism and foreshadowing, of salient elements in the environment. If this is the case, what happens with Madame Aubain's barometer? Should we conclude that Flaubert has indulgently presented an unnecessary detail that only distracts us from the story?

---

7   Valentine Tschebotarioff Bill, *Chekhov: The Silent Voice of Freedom* (New York, NY: Philosophical Library, 1987).

According to Barthes, one possible explanation is that the barometer is there, not to perform any specific function for setting, plot, or characterisation, but simply to reinforce the verisimilitude of the story.[8]

Verisimilitude (from the Latin 'truth-likeness') is the attempt by narrative discourse to convince readers that the storyworld is a faithful imitation or representation of the 'real' world. A verisimilar story is one that looks as if it could be true, regardless of whether it is true or not. We call nonfiction a story that claims to be true. But nonfiction narratives, even when they are true, can still fail to be verisimilar if they seem unbelievable to readers. Similarly, fictional stories, which do not pretend to be true, may or may not seem true to the reader (Fig. 3.8).

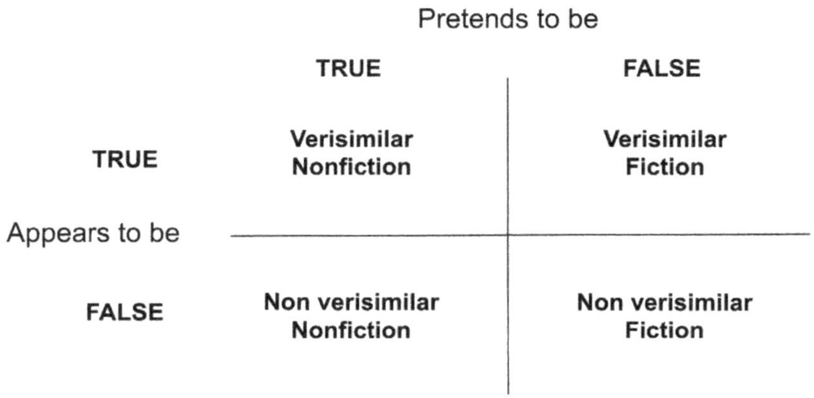

	Pretends to be TRUE	Pretends to be FALSE
Appears to be TRUE	Verisimilar Nonfiction	Verisimilar Fiction
Appears to be FALSE	Non verisimilar Nonfiction	Non verisimilar Fiction

Fig. 3.8 Schema of verisimilitude in fiction and nonfiction. By Ignasi Ribó, CC BY.

Madame Aubain's barometer, like other insignificant details of setting often found in literary descriptions, might just function as a reminder that the environment represented, while being fictitious, could be a real one. Just as our own rooms and offices are filled with objects that serve no purpose, adding these 'useless details' to the setting would encourage readers to willingly suspend their disbelief[9] and submerge themselves in the storyworld 'as if' it were the real one.

Summary

- All narratives build an alternative storyworld, which includes, besides other existents, one or more environments. An environment is everything that surrounds characters, wherever events take place.

---

8   Barthes, pp. 141–48.
9   Samuel Taylor Coleridge, *Biographia Literaria, or, Biographical Sketches of My Literary Life and Opinions*, ed. by James Engell and Walter Jackson Bate (Princeton, NJ: Princeton University Press, 1984).

- The arrangement of the environments of the story is called the setting, which may involve laying out artificial and natural things in space (topography) or establishing meaningful relationships between things and the actions, experiences, emotions, or thoughts of characters (atmosphere).

- In prose fiction we can identify four basic kinds of setting: irrelevant, functional, mental, and symbolic.

- Writers represent setting by providing long or short descriptions, which often include significant details that associate environments with characters and events, while helping readers to recreate them in their imagination.

- Descriptions can also include insignificant details about the environment in order to create an effect of reality and enhance the verisimilitude of the storyworld.

References

Bakhtin, Mikhail M., *The Dialogic Imagination: Four Essays*, trans. by Michael Holquist and Caryl Emerson (Austin, TX: University of Texas Press, 2011).

Barthes, Roland, *The Rustle of Language* (Berkeley, CA: University of California Press, 1989).

Bill, Valentine Tschebotarioff, *Chekhov: The Silent Voice of Freedom* (New York, NY: Philosophical Library, 1987).

Coleridge, Samuel Taylor, *Biographia Literaria, or, Biographical Sketches of My Literary Life and Opinions*, ed. by James Engell and Walter Jackson Bate (Princeton, NJ: Princeton University Press, 1984).

Herman, David, *Basic Elements of Narrative* (Chichester, UK: Wiley-Blackwell, 2009), https://doi.org/10.1002/9781444305920

Ryan, Marie-Laure, *Possible Worlds, Artificial Intelligence, and Narrative Theory* (Bloomington, IN: Indiana University Press, 1991).

Strunk, William, and E. B. White, *The Elements of Style* (Boston, MA: Allyn and Bacon, 1999).

Tuan, Yi-Fu, *Space and Place: The Perspective of Experience* (Minneapolis, MN: University of Minnesota Press, 2011).

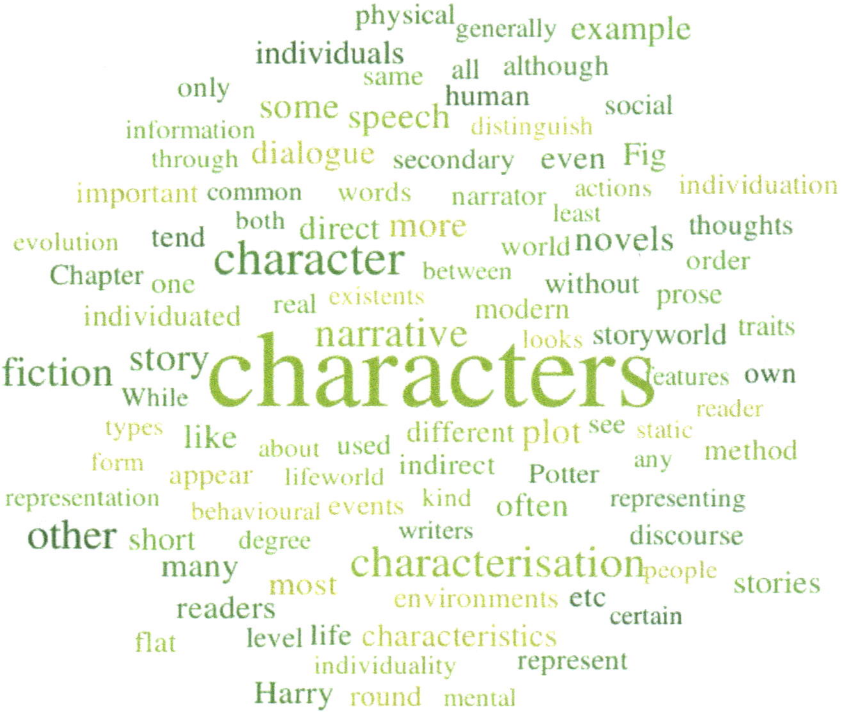
physical generally example
individuals
same all although
only human
some speech social
information distinguish
through dialogue secondary even Fig
important common words narrator actions individuation
least
evolution tend both direct more thoughts
character world novels
order
Chapter one between without
real existents prose
individuated modern
narrative traits
looks storyworld
fiction story characters features own
While reader
types like different plot see static
about used method
form any
appear lifeworld indirect Potter
representation behavioural events kind often representing
writers
other short degree discourse
many characterisation people stories
most
environments etc
readers certain
flat level life characteristics
individuality represent
Harry round mental

4. Characterisation

The worlds of prose fiction are not only made of events arranged into plots and environments arranged into settings. In order to have a story, there must also be characters. The arrangement of characters in the story is called characterisation. But what are characters? Why are they so necessary for narrative? What kinds of characters do we find in fiction stories? How are they characterised and represented? These are some of the questions that will occupy us in this last chapter dedicated to the elements of story.

A character is any entity in the story that has agency, that is, who is able to act in the environments of the storyworld. Characters are most often individuals (e.g. Ivan Karamazov in *The Brothers Karamazov*, Werther in *The Sorrows of Young Werther*, or Henry Jekyll in *Dr Jekyll and Mr Hyde*), but there are some special cases where we find collective or choral characters (e.g. Thebans in *Oedipus Rex*, or the group of neighbourhood boys in *The Virgin Suicides*). Characters are most often human beings, but they can also be nonhuman animals or other entities who behave like humans (e.g. the White Rabbit in *Alice in Wonderland* — Figure 4.1 — or the robots in *I, Robot*). Only exceptionally are the characters of short stories and novels animals or other entities without human features (e.g. the white whale in *Moby Dick*, or the aliens in *2001: A Space Odyssey*). In our discussion of character, therefore, we will assume that the characters of the story are human or human-like individuals, although there are notable exceptions to this rule.

That characters are important for narrative fiction can be seen from the fact that the titles of many short stories and novels are taken from the proper names of their main characters (protagonists). These are sometimes called eponymous characters and are very frequent in the history of literature. Some of the most famous novels are named after their protagonists, such as *Don Quixote*, *Robinson Crusoe*, *Jane Eyre*, *Madame Bovary*, or *Anna Karenina*. Even when characters do not appear in the title, they are still the most relevant existents in a great majority of short stories and novels. This seems to be a consequence of the nature and function

© Ignasi Ribó, CC BY 4.0   https://doi.org/10.11647/OBP.0187.04

Fig. 4.1
Illustration of Lewis Carroll *Alice in Wonderland* (1865). By John Tenniel, Public Domain, https://en.wikipedia.org/wiki/Alice%27s_Adventures_in_Wonderland#/media/File:Alice_par_John_Tenniel_02.png

of narrative. As we saw in the introduction, narrative is fundamentally a way for us humans to give meaning to our own world. And what is more important for us than ourselves and other entities like us?

While recognising the relevance of characters in narrative, we should not forget the intimate connections between characters and the other two existents of the story, events and environments (see Fig. 3.1, in Chapter 3). Stories are not simply made of characters acting in an environment. All the existents of the story are equally indispensable to the recreation of a convincing storyworld, just as they are in our own lifeworld. Thus, characterisation, plot, and setting need to work together in order to effectively sustain narrative discourse and contribute to meaningful communication between authors and readers.

In this chapter, we will start by discussing how the nature of characters changes when we analyse them at the level of narrative, discourse, or story. We will then consider the notion of individuation in order to show that characterisation in prose fiction is generally aimed at constructing fully individuated characters, but very often also produces typical and universal characters. When analysing fictional characters in psychological/realistic terms, it is common to distinguish their degree of individuation (flat vs. round characters), as well as their degree of personal development throughout the plot (static vs. dynamic characters). After looking at these typologies of character, we will discuss the most common approaches to representing them in narrative: indirect and direct characterisation. An important method of direct characterisation is dialogue, which will be the topic of the last section in this chapter.

4.1 The Actants of Narrative

The nature of characters varies depending on what level of the semiotic model we position ourselves in (see Figs. 1.5 and 1.7 in Chapter 1). At the level of narrative, characters may be seen as figments of the author, who endows them with certain features or qualities drawn from his imagination or observations, which are then recreated by readers in every reading. At the level of discourse, however, we can see characters as a construct of the text, a sort of 'paper people' whose features are exclusively constituted by the descriptions found in the text and the inferences that can be made from textual cues.[1] In this sense, characters are incomplete creatures, mere actants with no life beyond the text and no reason to exist other than to fulfil their function in the plot.[2] Harry Potter, for example, might appear as an almost real individual for many readers, but at the level of discourse he is simply the hero of an adventure story whose 'life' does not extend beyond the events narrated in the eponymous novels.

Things look different when we analyse characters as existents of the story. At that level, characters may be seen as individuals who inhabit an alternative world, the storyworld. It is a matter of some debate whether the existence of characters in the alternative world of the story should be regarded as complete or limited to text-based inferences. Here, we will assume that characters are endowed with at least a potentially complete existence in the storyworld. Of course, this existence is ultimately dependent on the narrator of the story (a figure of discourse). But within the confines of the storyworld created by narrative discourse, characters are generally agents endowed with an identity, social and personal relationships, feelings, desires and thoughts, just like any of us in our own lifeworld. Thus, Harry Potter might not be, nor could ever be, a real person in the world of its readers. But, in the storyworld created by J. K. Rowling's novels, he is a heroic and charismatic young wizard, with a multifaceted life, which includes the adventures narrated in the plots of the novels, but also, at least potentially, many other events, big and small, of which we may never hear.

As existents in the storyworld, all characters have in principle the same importance. In J. K. Rowling's fictional world, to continue

---

1   Uri Margolin, 'Character,' in *The Cambridge Companion to Narrative*, ed. by David Herman (Cambridge, UK: Cambridge University Press, 2007), pp. 66–79, https://doi.org/10.1017/ccol0521856965
2   Algirdas Julien Greimas and Joseph Courtés, *Semiotics and Language: An Analytical Dictionary*, trans. by Larry Crist and Daniel Patte (Bloomington, IN: Indiana University Press, 1982), pp. 5–8.

with the same example, Harry is not more important than Hermione Granger or Neville Longbottom. But narrative discourse, by arranging events, environments, and characters into a plot, necessarily establishes distinctions amongst the characters, just as it does amongst the events and environments. Thus, Harry Potter becomes much more relevant than all the other characters, taking on the role of the main character (the protagonist or hero) in the story, while the rest appear as secondary characters. Some of these secondary characters, like Hermione or Ron, have a very prominent role next to Harry, while many others, like Angelina Johnson or Bertha Jorkins, only appear fleetingly and play minor supporting roles in the plot. A few other characters from this storyworld, like Draco Malfoy or Dolores Umbridge, are cast as antagonists to Harry and his friends in the conflicts that drive the plot of the novels, even if, under a different arrangement of events and environments, they might have been cast in a different role.

4.2 Individuation

Whether characters are central to the story or only play a secondary role, their characterisation generally requires the narrator to directly or indirectly ascribe to them certain characteristics or properties that identify them as individuals. This is what we call individuation. In principle, a primary character will be more individuated than a secondary one. And we can expect the characters that are least relevant for the plot to be also the least individuated. But this rule has, in fact, notable exceptions. It is not uncommon to find secondary characters with characteristics so well defined that they become at least as individuated in the minds of the reader as the protagonist himself, if not more so. In Joseph Conrad's *Heart of Darkness*, for example, the elusive ivory trader Kurtz is characterised with more detail and nuance than Marlow, the protagonist of the story.

In general, individuation involves three sets of defining characteristics or traits:[3]

1. *Physical*: These are the features of the body, such as whether the character is tall or short, slim or fat, blue-eyed or brown-eyed, fair or dark, male or female, etc. Many physical characteristics are external and can be observed with the naked eye (e.g. the shape of the nose or a scar on the forehead), while others might be internal and thus difficult to perceive directly (e.g. diabetes or heartburn).

---

3   Uri Margolin, 'Individuals in Narrative Worlds: An Ontological Perspective,' *Poetics Today*, 11:4 (1990), 843–71.

2. *Mental*: These are the features of personality or psychology, such as whether the character is modest or arrogant, upbeat or depressive, cruel or kind, dreamy or practical, etc. These traits compose what is commonly understood as the character of a person. They might include traits that are perceptual (e.g. powers of observation), emotive (e.g. excitability), volitional (e.g. ambition), and cognitive (e.g. shrewdness).

3. *Behavioural*: These are the features of behaviour or habits, such as whether the character is punctual or unpunctual, shouts or whispers when speaking, laughs easily or never laughs at all, drinks or avoids alcohol, etc. Sometimes it is difficult to distinguish mental and behavioural traits, as they tend to be intimately connected. Behavioural traits may be related to any actions that characters undertake, including communicating and interacting with other characters.

The aim of individuation is to represent characters in such a way that they appear, speak, and act like real individuals. In the context of psychological or realistic fiction, a fully individuated character should be endowed with a particular set of physical, mental, and behavioural characteristics so as to allow readers to imagine him or her as a person living in the same kind of world in which we all live. Of course, storyworlds might be very different from our own lifeworld. It is possible, for example, to imagine a storyworld where individuality as we understand it does not exist and all 'individuals' are actually clones or genetic replicas of the same organism. In such a context, the notion of individuation would lose most of its sense. This kind of fiction, however, is notably difficult to create, precisely because individuality is such a central assumption in the worldview of both writers and readers.

As long as we stay within the boundaries of storyworlds that imitate, or are extrapolated from our own world, it makes sense to strive for individuality in characterisation. As social animals, we have evolved a set of perceptual and cognitive mechanisms that allow us to identify and distinguish other human individuals from each other. Given the importance of individuality for our own social existence, it is not surprising that our narratives should attempt to represent characters as plausible and self-standing individuals, endowing them with a distinctive set of characteristics.

Not all human cultures, however, give the same importance to individuality. We should not forget that modern novels and short stories are largely the products of the individualistic culture that emerged from the European Renaissance (see Chapter 1), closely associated with the scientific and industrial revolutions, the expansion of capitalism, and a philosophical conception of the human being as an isolated, autonomous, and self-reflecting individual. In this culture, which has now become globalised, narrative characters that are not fully individuated seem to lack something important, as if not being properly distinguishable from other characters would make them less real. This has not always been the case. In mythical narratives, for example, the characters are not so much individuals as types (e.g. the 'messenger') or universals (e.g. the 'hero'). Both typical and universal characters are still important in modern fiction, although their nature and function has been somewhat modified by the prevailing individualism of modern culture.

Fig. 4.2
Fan art representing Lord Voldemort and Nagini, from the Harry Potter saga, made with charcoal, acrylics and watercolours. By Mademoiselle Ortie aka Elodie Tihange, CC BY 4.0, https://fr.wikipedia.org/wiki/Fichier:Lord_Voldemort.jpg

Typical characters (or simply, types) represent a particular aspect of humanity or a particular group of humans. For example, characters representing evil in a concentrated and simplified form, like Lord Voldemort (Fig. 4.2), have become quite common in certain kinds of popular fiction. While these 'villains' might be individuated to a certain extent, they are not so much individuals as types. Many other typical characters, like the 'mad professor,' the 'femme fatale,' or the 'wise old man,' can be found in modern short stories and novels, where they tend to play secondary or supporting roles as stock characters. When types become ingrained in the psychology and culture of a society and start appearing in many different storyworlds, they are said to be archetypes.

In some respects, every character, no matter how well individuated, can be regarded as a type.[4] Even in real life we often perceive other individuals as types (e.g. immigrant, lawyer, Chinese, gay, nerd), a simplification that helps us to classify and group them into meaningful

---

4   H. Porter Abbott, *The Cambridge Introduction to Narrative* (Cambridge, UK: Cambridge University Press, 2008), pp. 129–31, https://doi.org/10.1017/cbo9780511816932

categories. This is the basis of prejudice and negative bias, but it is also an evolved mechanism to cope with complex social information. Similarly, characters in fiction, even those that have been individuated with the utmost craft, cannot avoid being cast as types by readers. Emma Bovary, the eponymous protagonist of Gustave Flaubert's novel *Madame Bovary*, is one of the characters of realist fiction that has been characterised with more detail and subtlety (see Fig. 4.3). And yet, she is often perceived as the typical adulterous woman, trying to balance the social imperatives of marriage with her romantic longings.

Fig. 4.3
'Madame Hessel en robe rouge lisant' (1905), oil on cardboard. By Édouard Vuillard, Public Domain, https://commons.wikimedia.org/wiki/File:%C3%89douard_Vuillard_-_Madame_Hessel_en_robe_rouge_lisant_(1905).jpg

Fig. 4.4 'Don Quixote and Sancho Panza at a crossroad,' oil on canvas. By Wilhelm Marstrand (1810–1873), CC0 1.0, https://commons.wikimedia.org/wiki/File:Wilhelm_Marstrand,_Don_Quixote_og_Sancho_Panza_ved_en_skillevej,_uden_datering_(efter_1847),_0119NMK,_Nivaagaards_Malerisamling.jpg

There are times when fictional characters are somehow able to transcend their individuality and typicality in order to attain some form of universality. Universal characters represent a general aspect of humanity or the whole human species. For example, Don Quixote and Sancho Panza, the protagonists of Cervantes' novel, have become a pair of universal characters, representing two fundamental and contrasting attitudes towards life that are generally found in human beings: idealism and materialism (Fig. 4.4). Similarly, in her desperate longing for a more fulfilling and authentic life, Emma Bovary may represent the alienation of all individuals in modern society, torn between reveries of plenitude and the unsatisfactory realities of everyday existence.

4.3 Kinds of Character

A certain number of typologies have been proposed to classify and distinguish analytically the kinds of character most often found in fiction. Two of these typologies are still used extensively by critics and writers, even though their psychological assumptions only make them applicable to realist fiction, that is, to storyworlds that attempt to imitate or replicate our own lifeworld.[5]

The first one of these typologies[6] distinguishes characters based on their degree of individuation:

1. *Flat characters*: These characters, which are sometimes equated to what we have called types in the previous section, are constructed around a limited number of traits or characteristics. Of course, there are varying degrees of flatness. At one extreme, we would find characters with a single characteristic or trait, such as a messenger whose only purpose in the story is to deliver a message at a certain point of the plot. Flat characters can be a bit more individuated than that, but their identity, personality, and purpose can often be expressed by a single sentence. They tend to lack depth or complexity and are easily recognisable and remembered by the reader. Because of their limited qualities, however, they also tend to seem quite artificial and most readers have a hard time identifying with them or taking them for real human beings. Minor or secondary characters in fiction tend to be flat, even when the main characters in the same story are not. In genres like comedy or adventure, flat characters are quite common. And some writers, like Charles Dickens or H. G. Wells,

---

5 See Seymour Benjamin Chatman, *Story and Discourse: Narrative Structure in Fiction and Film* (Ithaca, NY: Cornell University Press, 2000).
6 E. M. Forster, *Aspects of the Novel* (San Diego, CA: Harcourt Brace Jovanovich, 1985).

seemed quite inclined to populate their novels and short stories with flat secondary characters. An example of a flat character from the Harry Potter series is Argus Filch, the caretaker of Hogwarts, characterised almost exclusively by his love for cats and obsession with catching students who break the rules of the school (Fig. 4.5).

Fig. 4.5
Warner Bros. Studio Tour, London: The Making of Harry Potter. Source: Karen Roe, CC BY 2.0, https://commons.wikimedia.org/wiki/File:The_Making_of_Harry_Potter_29-05-2012_(7358054268).jpg

2. *Round characters*: These characters are endowed with many different traits or characteristics, some of which might even be contradictory and cause them internal or psychological conflicts. With well-crafted characterisation, round characters can appear to be as complex and multifaceted as any human being we might encounter in our world. Major characters in realist prose fiction, such as Emma Bovary, Rodion Raskolnikov, or Anna Karenina, are often round. And there are writers, like Gustave Flaubert or Jane Austen, who tend to characterise even minor characters with such nuance and complexity that they appear to be round, even though they might not have a prominent role in the story. An example of a round character in the Harry Potter novels is Hermione Granger, one of Harry's closest friends at Hogwarts. While roundness of character is the aim of many realist and popular stories, in modernist and postmodernist fiction the notion of character has often been questioned. In Robert Musil's novel *The Man Without Qualities*, for example, the main character is presented as devoid of any of those stable

characteristics, individual or typical, which would allow him to fit comfortably into the preconceived patterns of modern bourgeois society (Fig. 4.6).

Fig. 4.6
'Man without Qualities n°2' (2005), oil and metal on canvas. By Erik Pevernagie, CC BY-SA 4.0, https://commons.wikimedia.org/wiki/File:Man_without_Qualities_n%C2%B02.jpg

Another typology, also based on a psychological-realist conception of character and often confused with the previous one, distinguishes characters in terms of their ability to change or evolve throughout the plot:

1. *Static characters*: These characters do not experience any profound change or personal evolution from the moment they appear in the plot until they disappear. Most flat characters are also static, although these classifications are based on different variables. It is possible, although relatively unusual, to have a flat character whose limited characteristics undergo a radical transformation in the story. More common is to have round characters that are static, retaining the same personality, identity, or characteristics throughout the whole narrative. In the Harry Potter novels, for example, most major characters, including Harry, Ron, and Hermione, are fairly static, evolving only superficially from their initial appearance until the end of the series, even if the author has tried to add dynamism into their characterisation in order to take account of their growing up into adulthood.

2. *Dynamic characters*: These characters undergo profound and significant changes as the story develops, showing some degree of personal evolution or growth which transforms them into somewhat different characters at the end of the

plot. This evolution is not always positive or constructive, and the changes experienced by the character may involve different forms of crisis, physical or psychological degradation, depression, and other negative or destructive changes. Given their complexity and depth, round characters are generally more able to experience this kind of dynamism, although there are many cases where round characters remain static. In short stories, dynamic characters are far less common than in novels, where the length of the narrative provides more opportunities to show character development and evolution. To continue with examples from the Harry Potter novels, Neville Longbottom is one of the few characters who undergoes a significant evolution throughout the series, as he grows up and develops a more confident and bold personality.

4.4 Representing Characters

Like environments, characters in literary narrative need to be represented through words. They cannot be shown directly to the audience, as in film or drama. There are basically two ways to represent characters in prose fiction:[7]

1. *Indirect characterisation*: The character is presented by the narrator, who describes his or her physical, mental, or behavioural characteristics. Character descriptions are similar to environmental descriptions. They can be long and detailed or short and cursory. And they often rely on significant details that connect characters to the setting, the plot, or even the reader. In certain cases, some details in a character description might be unnecessary or insignificant, but they can serve to make the character seem more realistic. In indirect characterisation, the narrator also tends to use commentary to qualify or evaluate the character, providing a subjective interpretation that goes beyond mere description. Indirect characterisation has the advantage of conveying a lot of information about characters in a short time. But, as a form of 'telling' (see Chapter 5), it creates some distance between the reader and the character, making the latter less moving and memorable than when direct methods of characterisation are used.

2. *Direct characterisation*: The character is revealed through his or her actions, words, looks, thoughts, or effects on other

---

[7] Janet Burroway, *Writing Fiction: A Guide to Narrative Craft* (Chicago, IL: University of Chicago Press, 2019), https://doi.org/10.7208/chicago/9780226616728.001.0001

characters. Here, the narrator simply records external or internal events related to the character, including words and thoughts, without undertaking a descriptive summary or evaluation of the character's traits. Direct characterisation is, therefore, a form of 'showing' (see Chapter 5). It leaves the reader to interpret the character based on the information provided in the narrative. This kind of characterisation is more vivid and effective than the indirect method. But it also asks more from readers, who are required to participate in the construction of characters through their interpretations.

Both forms of characterisation are often used in short stories and novels. But direct characterisation is generally preferred in modern works of fiction, as it does not require the mediation of an intrusive narrative voice and allows characters to appear more like real people. There are five methods of direct characterisation that are commonly used in narrative: speech, thoughts, effects, actions, and looks. These can be easily remembered with the acronym STEAL.

1. *Speech*: What characters say and how they say it is one of the most important components of direct characterisation. Verbal language is the fundamental semiotic system that we humans employ to communicate meanings, emotions, intentions, and so on. When it involves an interaction with other people, we call this dialogue. In prose fiction, speech is a widely used method of characterisation, as it can be very effective in revealing explicit and implicit information about the characters engaged in dialogue. At the same time, speech can serve to move the plot forward and provide information about events, environments, or other characters in the storyworld.

2. *Thoughts*: Knowing what the characters think (or desire, want, plan, etc.) can also help to define their characteristics. Of course, in our lifeworld, we have no access to what other people think, except when they tell us about it. This is the reason why some modern writers try to avoid this method of characterisation, constraining the narrator to represent what can be observed from the outside, but never entering the characters' minds. However, in many other works of fiction, both classical and modern, readers are allowed access to the thoughts of at least some of the characters, which are necessarily expressed in words, as some form of interior speech or monologue. Modern writers often use more sophisticated techniques like free indirect speech or interior monologue (stream of consciousness) to try to

convey the complex and fluid mental processes of characters.[8] Molly Bloom's interior monologue at the end of James Joyce's *Ulysses* is perhaps the most famous example of this technique in modern literature.

3. *Effects*: How other characters are affected or react to a character can be used to characterise, not just those characters (using speech, thought, or action), but also the character that causes the effect. For example, if the characters surrounding John laugh every time he says or does something, readers will tend to assume that John is either funny or ridiculous. This is an effective characterisation technique because it replicates how we judge character in our own life. As social animals, we are always attentive to the impression people make on other people. For instance, we would tend to see as attractive someone at whom others stare with desire or interest, even without knowing what that person looks like.

4. *Actions*: What characters do, their behaviour, is perhaps the most important method of direct characterisation. In general, actions often involve some kind of physical movement (e.g. gesturing, walking, running, etc.), but they can also be passive states (e.g. sleeping, sitting, etc.), or even internal changes reflected in the face or body of the character (e.g. staring, frowning, etc.). Nonverbal communication, which usually accompanies and supports dialogue, is based on actions. Since the characters in fiction are almost always doing something as part of the plot, every action is an opportunity to characterise them in one way or another in the mind of the reader. This is also how we judge each other in life, not only by our words, but also by our deeds.

5. *Looks*: How a character looks or appears in the story can also be a useful method of direct characterisation. Appearance includes the physical traits of the character's face and body (e.g. eye colour, hair length, height, skin complexion, etc.), but also their way of dressing or presenting themselves in front of others. In our lifeworld, appearance provides important cues about a person's social status, occupation, mental and physical state, intentions and thoughts, etc. In prose fiction, looks are often employed to provide the same kind of information, typically through some form of description. In some cases, it can be

---

8   Dorrit Cohn, *Transparent Minds: Narrative Modes for Presenting Consciousness in Fiction* (Princeton, NJ: Princeton University Press, 1988).

difficult to distinguish between descriptions that use indirect characterisation (presented from the subjective perspective of the narrator) and those that use direct characterisation (without any subjective intervention by the narrator).

4.5 Dialogue

In narrative, the representation of communicative interaction using speech, or dialogue, contributes both to the development of plot and to the characterisation of characters. It can also help to establish the setting, for example through the representation of different dialects or ways of speaking. It is thus a crucial resource used in many short stories and novels, although the importance of dialogue and the techniques employed to convey it vary quite substantially from one narrative to another.

By far the most common method of representing dialogue in prose fiction is direct speech, where the words spoken by the characters appear transcribed and enclosed in quotation marks or other conventional signs. Sometimes, the characters' words are accompanied with dialogue (or speech) tags that indicate who is speaking and provide other relevant information about the interaction (e.g. '"How could I suspect she wanted to kill me?," said the detective, still shaking his head.'). This method of representing dialogue introduces a dramatic element into the narrative, providing the reader of prose fiction with an experience that approaches that of watching a play or a film.

While many authors attempt to write realistic dialogue that captures the quality and structure of spoken interaction, the truth is that narrative dialogue is subject to many conventions and must be stylised in order to be intelligible for readers. Conversations in real life are full of fragments, repetitions, meaningless sounds, nonverbal cues, gaps, lapses, pauses, etc. But narrative representations of dialogue are often tidied up to provide an idealised and artificial version of conversation, in order to create the impression of reality without wearing down or losing the interest of readers.[9]

There are other methods to convey dialogue in narrative, although they tend to lack the immediacy and effectiveness of direct speech. In indirect speech, for example, the narrator reports the words of a character without quoting them directly (e.g. 'The detective claimed that he never suspected his girlfriend wanted to kill him.'). Free indirect speech (or free indirect style) can also serve to report spoken words, although it is more commonly used to convey the character's thoughts. This method

---

[9] Norman Page, *Speech in the English Novel* (London, UK: Macmillan, 1988).

combines the narrator's third-person narration with the essence of the character's first-person speech, without using quotation marks (e.g. 'The detective shook his head when he found out. How could he ever suspect that his girlfriend wanted to kill him?').

Regardless of the actual method used to represent speech and conversation, there is little doubt that dialogue and, in general, the representation of different voices and perspectives, is a fundamental principle of modern prose fiction. As the literary theorist Mikhail Bakhtin pointed out in his analysis of Dostoevsky's narratives (Fig. 4.7), many novels tend to be 'polyphonic,' that is, they combine, without merging them, 'a plurality of consciousnesses, with equal rights and each with its own world.'[10] The 'dialogic principle'[11] brings together voices from a multiplicity of social and ideological worlds (including the voices of the different characters, the voices of narrators, and even voices external to the story itself) in order to create a narrative that aspires to be as rich and multifarious as life itself.

Fig. 4.7
Portrait of Fyodor Dostoevsky by Vasily Petrov (1872). Tretyakov Gallery, Public Domain, https://commons.wikimedia.org/wiki/Фёдор_Михайлович_Достоевский#/media/File:Dostoevsky_1872.jpg

---

10 Mikhail M. Bakhtin, *Problems of Dostoevsky's Poetics*, ed. by Caryl Emerson (Minneapolis, MN: University of Minnesota Press, 1984), p. 6.

11 Mikhail M. Bakhtin, *The Dialogic Imagination: Four Essays*, trans. by Michael Holquist and Caryl Emerson (Austin, TX: University of Texas Press, 2011).

Summary

- At the level of discourse, characters are mere actants with no features other than those defined in the text and no reason for being other than their function in the plot. At the level of story, however, we can regard them as existents of the storyworld.

- In realist prose fiction, characterisation aims to individuate characters by ascribing to them physical, mental, and behavioural characteristics or properties that distinguish them as individuals.

- Most characters can be classified according to their degree of individuation (flat vs. round) or their degree of personal evolution throughout the plot (static vs. dynamic).

- The representation of characters in short stories and novels is generally achieved through indirect or direct methods of characterisation. Direct methods involve the representation of characters' speech, thoughts, effects (on other characters), actions, or looks.

- In prose fiction, dialogue (the representation of speech interactions between characters) is usually an important element of the story, contributing both to emplotment and characterisation.

References

Abbott, H. Porter, *The Cambridge Introduction to Narrative* (Cambridge, UK: Cambridge University Press, 2008), https://doi.org/10.1017/cbo9780511816932

Bakhtin, Mikhail M., *Problems of Dostoevsky's Poetics*, ed. by Caryl Emerson (Minneapolis, MN: University of Minnesota Press, 1984).

Bakhtin, Mikhail M., *The Dialogic Imagination: Four Essays*, trans. by Michael Holquist and Caryl Emerson (Austin, TX: University of Texas Press, 2011).

Burroway, Janet, *Writing Fiction: A Guide to Narrative Craft* (Chicago, IL: University of Chicago Press, 2019), https://doi.org/10.7208/chicago/9780226616728.001.0001

Chatman, Seymour Benjamin, *Story and Discourse: Narrative Structure in Fiction and Film* (Ithaca, NY: Cornell University Press, 2000).

Cohn, Dorrit, *Transparent Minds: Narrative Modes for Presenting Consciousness in Fiction* (Princeton, NJ: Princeton University Press, 1988).

Forster, E. M., *Aspects of the Novel* (San Diego, CA: Harcourt Brace Jovanovich, 1985).

Greimas, Algirdas Julien, and Joseph Courtés, *Semiotics and Language: An Analytical Dictionary*, trans. by Larry Crist and Daniel Patte (Bloomington, IN: Indiana University Press, 1982).

Margolin, Uri, 'Character', in *The Cambridge Companion to Narrative*, ed. by David Herman (Cambridge, UK: Cambridge University Press, 2007), pp. 66–79, https://doi.org/10.1017/ccol0521856965

Margolin, Uri, 'Individuals in Narrative Worlds: An Ontological Perspective,' *Poetics Today*, 11:4 (1990), 843–71.

Page, Norman, *Speech in the English Novel* (London, UK: Macmillan, 1988).

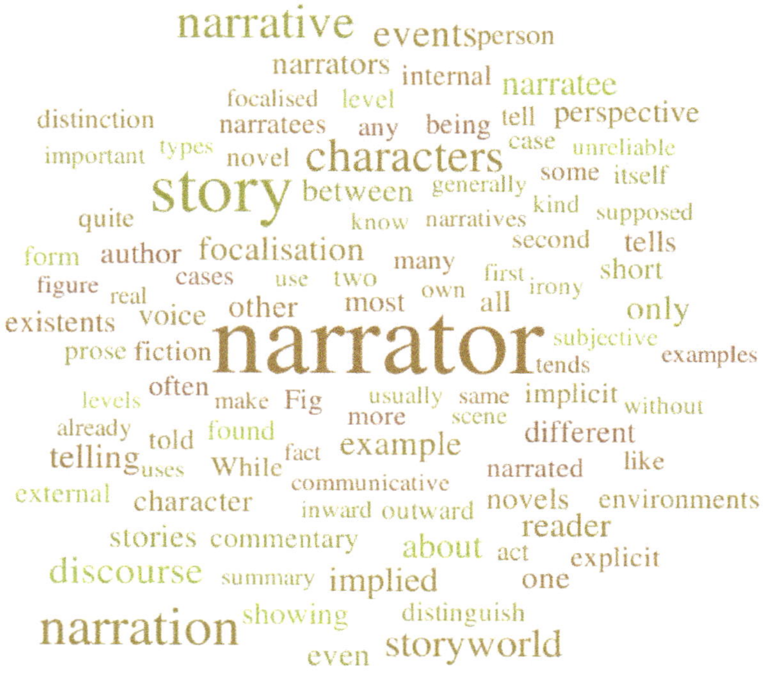
narrative
events
person
narrators
internal
narratee
focalised
level
distinction
narratees
any
being
tell
perspective
important
types
novel
characters
case
unreliable
story
between
generally
some
itself
quite
know
narratives
kind
supposed
form
author
focalisation
many
second
tells
figure
cases
use
two
first
short
real
own
irony
existents
voice
other
most
all
only
prose
fiction
narrator
subjective
tends
examples
levels
often
make
Fig
usually
same
implicit
without
already
more
scene
told
found
example
different
telling
uses
While
fact
narrated
like
communicative
external
character
inward
outward
novels
environments
reader
stories
commentary
about
act
explicit
discourse
summary
implied
one
narration
showing
distinguish
even
storyworld

5. Narration

So far, we have been analysing the main constituents of the story, or, as we have called them, the existents of the storyworld: events, environments, and characters. But the storyworld only comes to exist because someone (a narrator) tells a story to someone else (a narratee). This is what we call narration, a communicative act that does not happen in the storyworld or at the level of the story. Narration is part of discourse, which constitutes the second level in our semiotic model of narrative.

Narrative discourse is basically the communication between the implied author and the implied reader of a narrative (see Fig. 1.5, Chapter 1). The 'implied author'[1] is implied because it does not have an explicit or independent reality, as the real author does, but must be reconstructed by the reader from the narrative itself. It is important in this sense to distinguish the implied author from the narrator of the story. The implied author does not tell anything; it does not have a voice, but it is simply the organising principle of discourse, which includes the narrator and the other aspects of the narration.[2] Every narrative has an implied author, even if it does not have a real author (e.g. a computer-generated text) or it has many of them (e.g. collaborative fiction). Similarly, every narrative has an implied reader, which is the ideal reader addressed by narrative discourse.[3]

In this chapter, we will examine in some detail the different elements of narration. Then, in the next chapters, we will look at other key aspects of discourse, namely language and theme. Of course, the questions raised by the analysis of discourse often cross over to the story. Therefore, we must always keep in mind the distinction between these two levels of narrative.

---

1 Wayne C. Booth, *The Rhetoric of Fiction* (Chicago, IL: University of Chicago Press, 1983).
2 Seymour Benjamin Chatman, *Story and Discourse: Narrative Structure in Fiction and Film* (Ithaca, NY: Cornell University Press, 2000), pp. 147–51.
3 Wolfgang Iser, *The Implied Reader: Patterns of Communication in Prose Fiction from Bunyan to Beckett* (Baltimore, MD: Johns Hopkins University Press, 1995).

© Ignasi Ribó, CC BY 4.0   https://doi.org/10.11647/OBP.0187.05

This is particularly important when we discuss narration, because the object of narration is the story itself. We can only interpret the storyworld (with all its events, environments, and characters) from the story told by the narrator to the narratee. While neither the narrator nor the narratee need to exist as such in the storyworld, these figures of discourse can also be characters in the story, a complication that we will try to clarify in the following pages.

First, we need to define more precisely what we mean by narration and the relationship between narration and the story being narrated. Then we will look more closely at the two figures of discourse involved in narration, the narrator and the narratee, outlining the types most commonly found in prose fiction. We will then examine the concept of focalisation, an important and closely related aspect of narration, which refers to the point of view or perspective adopted by the narrator of the story. Next, we will discuss in more detail the basic means by which narrators can represent events, characters, and environments: telling and showing. But narrators, besides representing the existents of the storyworld, often also make comments about them. To conclude the chapter, therefore, we will consider the use of explicit and implicit commentary in prose fiction.

5.1 The Expression of Narrative

Narration is the communicative act of telling a story. The figures of discourse involved in this act are the narrator (who tells the story) and the narratee (who listens to, or reads, the story). The story is what is being told. Narration is how it is being told. This involves a series of prior decisions, attributed to the implied author (and, ultimately, to the real author), about who the narrator will be, what kind of knowledge the narrator will have about the existents of the storyworld, what narrative techniques the narrator will employ to convey the story, etc. All these decisions, taken together, define the expression of narrative, that is, the process of communicating the story.

Here, we are mostly concerned with the narration of a story, which is an instance of narrative discourse. But prose fiction can also include narration within the story itself.[4] For example, in *One Thousand and One Nights* a narrator tells the story of a sultan who kills all of his new wives after the first night, until Scheherazade keeps him in suspense for 1,001 nights by telling him different stories (see Fig. 5.1). The narrator of these stories is of course Scheherazade herself. But many of the stories she tells include characters who tell other stories in their turn. The result is

---

4 Shlomith Rimmon-Kenan, *Narrative Fiction: Contemporary Poetics* (London, UK: Routledge, 2002), pp. 94–97, https://doi.org/10.4324/9780203426111

an intricate structure of embedded or subordinated narratives. While most short stories and novels are not as complex as *One Thousand and One Nights*, the technique of embedding narratives, also known as 'a story within a story,' is a relatively common literary device. Such a technique, however, does not affect the general framework of our semiotic model of narrative. Regardless of how many embedded stories we find in a narrative, every story is framed by a higher level of discourse, which includes its narration.[5] If that narration is part of another story, then the whole structure is repeated, until we reach the highest level of narrative, which links an implied author with an implied reader.

Fig. 5.1 Édouard Frédéric Wilhelm Richter, *Scheherazade* (before 1913), Public Domain, https://commons.wikimedia.org/wiki/File:Edouard_Frederic_Wilhelm_Richter_-_Scheherazade.jpg

In some cases, short stories and novels consciously play with the different levels of narrative, in order to transgress them or simply for comic effect. For example, Laurence Sterne's novel *Tristram Shandy* is narrated by the eponymous character, who is supposed to tell his life story. But the narrator constantly crosses the boundaries of narration in order to directly address the reader or to call into question the verisimilitude of the narrative itself. In postmodernist fiction of the late twentieth century, there are quite a few examples of this sort of transgression, often using the so-called '*mise en abyme*' device, in which the technique of embedding

---

5 See Gérard Genette, *Narrative Discourse: An Essay in Method* (Ithaca, NY: Cornell University Press, 1990), pp. 25–32.

stories within stories creates unresolvable paradoxes, as in André Gide's *The Counterfeiters*, where one of the characters intends to write the same novel in which he appears.

All these self-conscious devices, rather than contradicting the general framework of narrative that we have been presenting here, are exceptions that confirm the rule. The fact is that most fictions establish, explicitly or implicitly, a clear distinction between the level of discourse and the level of story. Narration, which occurs at the level of discourse, is the communicative act between a narrator and a narratee responsible for expressing or representing all the elements of the story.

5.2 Narrators and Narratees

The narrator of a story is the figure of discourse that tells the story. This definition seems simple enough, but in practice there are several complications. Similarly, the narratee is the figure of discourse to whom the narrator tells the story. Again, there are quite a few practical considerations about this figure that we need to clarify.

In most short stories and novels, the narrator can be easily identified by asking the question: 'who speaks?' (or 'who writes?' when the story is supposedly told in writing). Very often, however, this narrator does not have a name or a clear identity, so we speak of an unknown narrator, even though we can sometimes infer details about his or her life, personality, or opinions from the narration itself. In other cases, the narrator is just a voice with no subjective dimension whatsoever.

One aspect of this voice that is usually obvious from the narrative is the so-called person. Founded on a grammatical distinction, the notion of person allows us to discern the underlying relationships between the narrator, the narratee, and the characters in the story:

1. *First-person narrator*: The narrator tends to use the first person quite often ('I went out at five o'clock.'), even if other grammatical persons can also be used. This kind of narrative voice is commonly found in stories told by a narrator who is also the protagonist, or at least a relevant character, in the plot. The narratee may or may not be explicit. For example, J. D. Salinger's *The Catcher in the Rye* (Fig. 5.2) is narrated by its seventeen-year-old protagonist, Holden Caulfield, who naturally tends to talk quite a lot about himself.

2. *Second-person narrator*: The narrator uses the second person most of the time ('You went out at five o'clock.'). The second person explicitly refers to the narratee, which in some cases might be the narrator himself. This kind of voice is difficult to sustain

Fig. 5.2
First-edition cover of *The Catcher in the Rye* (1951) by J. D. Salinger, Public Domain, https://commons.wikimedia.org/wiki/File:The_Catcher_in_the_Rye_(1951,_first_edition_cover).jpg

throughout the narrative, and has generally been tried only in experimental novels, such as Italo Calvino's *If on a Winter's Night a Traveller*, where the framing narrative directly addresses a reader of the novel (narratee).

3. *Third-person narrator*: The narrator uses the third person most of the time ('The marquise went out at five o'clock.'). This is, by far, the most common narrative person in prose fiction. The narrator may or may not be a character in the story. Similarly, the narratee may be explicit or implicit. There are countless examples of this kind of person. One of them is John Steinbeck's *The Grapes of Wrath*, told by a narrator who does not participate in the story.

It is also important to make a distinction, somewhat related to the previous classification, between two kinds of narrators:

1. *External narrator*: The narrator only exists as a figure of discourse. She is not a character in the story and only speaks from outside of the storyworld. Once again, *The Grapes of Wrath* is a good example of this type of narrator.

2. *Internal narrator*: An internal narrator, on the other hand, besides being a figure of discourse, is also an existent in the storyworld. Whether he is actually a character depends on his participation in the story, which can be extensive (e.g. a narrator who is also a major character, like the husband in Raymond Carver's short story 'Cathedral'), or limited (e.g. a narrator who is just a secondary character, like Dr Watson in 'A Scandal in Bohemia' and many other Sherlock Holmes stories). While

it is also possible for the narrator to be part of the storyworld without being a character in the story, this is quite rare and, for all practical purposes, not easy to distinguish from an external narrator.

There are also certain types of narrative that seem to lack a narrator, for example epistolary novels like Pierre Choderlos de Laclos' *Les Liaisons dangereuses*, which is entirely made up of letters exchanged between the different characters. But even in such cases there is an implicit figure of discourse, a narrator, who has arranged and edited the letters to tell a certain story. What is lacking here, therefore, is not the narrator, but the narrative voice or an explicit narration.

Finally, we should not forget that narration is itself a process, a communicative act carried out by a narrator at a certain time and place. The spatial relationship between the narrator's environment and the environments of the storyworld is usually only relevant if the narrator is internal to the storyworld. But the temporal relationship between narration and the events of the story has some influence on the form of narrative discourse, even if the temporalities of the narrator and the storyworld belong to different levels. When considered in relation to the events arranged in the plot, there are basically three kinds of narration:[6]

1. *Ulterior narration*: Events are supposed to have already happened when the narrator tells the story. This is the most common form of narration, which uses past tense as a standard narrative tense. Most short stories and novels are narrated using this convention.

2. *Anterior narration*: Events are not supposed to have happened yet when the narrator tells the story. This form, which tends to use the future tense, is quite rare in prose fiction. We generally only find it in prophecy or visionary narratives, for example in the Bible.

3. *Simultaneous narration*: Events are supposed to happen while the narrator tells the story. This form is usually only found in diaries or novels that experiment with narrative voice, as in Michel Butor's *Second Thoughts*, narrated in present tense and addressed by the narrator to himself.

As with any communicative act, narration involves a sender, the narrator, but also a recipient, the narratee. The narratee is situated at the same level as the narrator. But narratees are generally not as easy to identify as narrators. While they are sometimes explicitly mentioned in the narrative, most often they are only implicit figures, never mentioned or even acknowledged.

---

6   Rimmon-Kenan, pp. 90–102.

Like narrators, narratees can be external or internal to the storyworld. External narratees are generally left implicit and could easily be mistaken for implied or real readers. Even when the narrator addresses the narratee as 'reader,' for example in Charlotte Brontë's novel *Jane Eyre*, it does not mean that she is in fact addressing the real (or even the implied) reader. In this case, the label 'reader' is simply the term employed by the narrator to address an otherwise undetermined external narratee. Certainly, it seems that the (implied) author has chosen to put in the mouth of the narrator a term that refers to the (implied) reader. But such transgression of the levels of narrative (see Chapter 1) is only superficial. In fact, the narrator of a story can never address the implied reader, which is necessarily external to the discourse that brings the narrator herself into existence.

Internal narratees can also be left implicit, in which case it is difficult to distinguish them from external ones. When they are identified during the narration, internal narratees tend to be minor characters (e.g. the stranger who listens to the story told by Jean-Baptiste Clamence in Albert Camus' *The Fall*) or other existents in the storyworld (e.g. the unnamed individual to whom the narrator of Edgar Allan Poe's 'The Tell-Tale Heart' addresses his plea). There are also instances of collective narratees, when the narrator addresses an audience instead of a single recipient (e.g. the sailors who listen to Marlow's story in *The Heart of Darkness* or the academic public of the ape Red Peter in Kafka's 'A Report to an Academy'), as well as cases where the narrator and the narratee are identical, for example when the story is narrated in an intimate diary (e.g. Helen Fielding's *Bridget Jones's Diary*).

Finally, we should not forget that narration in prose fiction is sometimes shared by multiple narrators and can address multiple narratees, with the different parts of the narrative presented as a sequence of chapters, as in William Faulkner's *The Sound and the Fury*, or intertwined in more complex arrangements, as in Vladimir Nabokov's *Pale Fire*.

5.3 Focalisation

Identifying the narrator of a story is generally not enough to properly understand the mechanism of narration. Some narrators seem to move in and out of different characters' consciousness with ease, while others remain attached to a single character's perspective or constrain themselves to narrating observable events, without ever penetrating any character's consciousness or presuming to know their thoughts. These differences can be better grasped with the concept of focalisation, a technical term that is commonly used in narratology to replace the more ambiguous, but still popular, concept of point of view.

If the response to the question 'who speaks?' in a narrative is 'the narrator,' focalisation responds to the additional question 'from which perspective or point of view?' Focalisation can be defined as the perspective adopted by the narrator when telling the story, which is basically determined by the position of the narrator in relation to the characters in the storyworld. We can identify two fundamental types of focalisation:[7]

1. *Inward focalisation*: The narrator tells the story from the subjective perspective of a focal character, revealing her inner thoughts and feelings as if he could somehow enter inside or read her mind. In the case of a first-person narrator, of course, focalisation tends to be inward, even if the narrator might be speaking from the perspective of his younger or infant self, as in many autobiographical narratives, such as Charles Dickens' *Great Expectations*. A third-person narrator, even one that is external to the storyworld, can also be inwardly focalised, when he adopts or tells the story from the subjective perspective of one of the characters. A classic example is Henry James's novel *The Ambassadors*, narrated by an external narrator from the perspective or point of view of its protagonist, Lambert Strether.

2. *Outward focalisation*: The narrator tells the story without presuming to know or have access to the subjective perspective of any character, simply reporting what can be observed from the outside. When the narrator is internal to the storyworld, even if she doesn't participate directly in the events of the story, outward focalisation usually involves a certain degree of subjectivity, given that the narrator herself is a focal character. It is difficult in those cases to determine with precision whether the narration is outwardly or inwardly focalised. If the narrator is external, on the other hand, it is much simpler to sustain an outwardly focalised narration, where the narrator acts like a camera, recording everything that happens in the storyworld without entering the consciousness of any of the characters. Examples of this type of focalisation can be found in Dashiell Hammett's detective novels and short stories, such as *The Maltese Falcon* (Fig. 5.3).

Inward and outward focalisation may be fixed throughout the narrative, as in the examples provided above. But focalisation can also be variable, for example when the narrator alternates between inward and outward

---

[7] Based on Genette, pp. 189–211.

Fig. 5.3 Promotional still from the 1941 film *The Maltese Falcon*, published in the *National Board of Review Magazine*, p. 12. L-R: Humphrey Bogart, Mary Astor, Barton MacLane, Peter Lorre, and Ward Bond, Public Domain, https://commons.wikimedia.org/wiki/File:Maltese-Falcon-Tell-the-Truth-1941.jpg

focalisations (e.g. Stendhal's *The Red and the Black*), or multiple, when the narrator uses different focal characters to tell the story (e.g. George R. R. Martin's *A Song of Ice and Fire*).

Another important aspect of narration, which is related (and often confused) with focalisation, is the degree of knowledge that the narrator has about the existents of the storyworld, in particular about the inner thoughts and feelings of the characters. Here, we are implicitly asking the question 'how much does the narrator know?' In this sense, we can distinguish three types of narrators:

1. *Omniscient*: The narrator is like a God of the storyworld, knowing everything about its existents, including the internal or psychological states of all characters and the unfolding of events. In this case, focalisation is often variable and multiple, changing from outward to inward and from one character to another as the narrator thinks appropriate, which might give the impression that there is in fact no focalisation at all. Many classic short stories and novels are narrated with this sort of God-like narrator, for example J. R. R. Tolkien's *The Lord of the Rings*.

2. *Limited*: The narrator has only limited knowledge about the internal or psychological states of one or some of the existents in the storyworld. This is quite common in inwardly focalised

fictions, where the narrator only knows what the focal character or characters think and perceive, while having no access to the consciousness of other characters. When the focal character is the narrator himself, as in first-person narratives, his perspective is generally limited. An example of this kind of narration may be found in Jorge Luís Borges's short story 'Funes the Memorious,' where an unnamed first-person narrator recounts his relationship with a man who remembers absolutely everything.

3. *Objective*: The narrator has no knowledge about the internal or psychological states of any of the characters in the storyworld and can only report what can be observed from the outside. The perspective of an objective narrator, which tends to be outwardly focalised, can be compared to that of a movie camera. While both the camera and the objective narrator need to select and frame their perceptions, they can only record what can be externally perceived in the storyworld, but not what characters think or feel. Ernest Hemingway's 'The Killers' is a minimalist short story about a pair of criminals in a restaurant which is narrated with this kind of camera-eye perspective.

5.4 Telling and Showing

Already established in Classical poetics, particularly by Plato and Aristotle, the distinction between 'telling' (*diegesis*) and 'showing' (*mimesis*) can help to clarify certain important aspects of narrative discourse. Telling refers to the representation of the story through the mediation of a narrator, who gives an account and often interprets or comments on the events, environments, or characters of the storyworld. Showing, on the other hand, is supposed to be the direct representation of the events, environments, and characters of the story without the intervention of a narrator, leaving readers or spectators to make their own inferences or interpretations.

The distinction between these two concepts is quite clear when we compare a story told by a third-person narrator (telling) and the same story represented as a dramatic play, with a stage imitating the environments, actors playing the characters, and events being enacted as if they were happening in the storyworld (showing). However, using this same pair of concepts to distinguish between different forms of narration is not so straightforward.

We have already seen that all narratives have a narrator, even if the narrator can adopt an outward focalisation (e.g. camera-eye perspective) or even lack a perceptible narrative voice (e.g. the editor of a set of letters).

In this sense, all narration is a form of telling (*diegesis*), not showing (*mimesis*). But we have also seen that there can be different forms of narration. In some cases, the narrator conveys the words of characters using his own voice, as in 'The detective claimed that he never suspected his girlfriend wanted to kill him.' In other cases, the narrator quotes the words that were supposedly spoken by the characters themselves, as in '"How could I suspect she wanted to kill me?" said the detective.' The first type of narration can be qualified as telling, while the second is a derived form of showing. In this case, the distinction is not based on the presence or absence of a narrator, but rather on his prominence or degree of involvement in the narration.

In prose fiction, telling and showing usually involve the use of two different narrative methods to represent the events of the plot:

1. *Summary*: A summary narrates events by compressing their duration. For example, a narrator might tell about a long war by saying: 'Battles were won and lost, many died, and at the end no one felt victorious.' A single sentence summarises years of war, with all its battles and other significant events. In general, summary brings narration closer to the ideal of telling. In the same way that description is the telling of environments and characters, summary is the telling of events.

Fig. 5.4 Theatre scene: two women making a call on a witch (all three of them wear theatre masks). Roman mosaic from the Villa del Cicerone in Pompeii, now in the Museo Archeologico Nazionale (Naples). By Dioscorides of Samos, Public Domain, https://commons.wikimedia.org/wiki/File:Pompeii_-_Villa_del_Cicerone_-_Mosaic_-_MAN.jpg

2. *Scene*: A scene narrates a sequence of events in enough detail to create the illusion that they are unfolding in front of the narratee (and ultimately, the reader). Usually, the illusion is created by quoting dialogue in direct speech, intersected with brief descriptions of the environment and the characters, as well as some narration of the characters' actions. This method, which is already found in Ancient epic, seems to be inspired by drama, which has traditionally been considered the most effective method of representing a story (see Fig. 5.4). Thus, scene brings narration closer to the ideal of showing.

Despite the recurrent debates that oppose telling to showing, the fact is that both forms of narration are commonly found in most short stories and novels. Neither of them is superior to the other, and both have their own uses and limitations.

5.5 Commentary

Narrative discourse can do more than just tell a story through the voice of a narrator. It can also contain commentary, which consists of any pronouncement of the narrator that goes beyond a description or account of the existents of the story. While commentary, like the rest of narration, is expressed by the narrator's voice, it can also include messages sent by the implied author to the implied reader through the narrator's voice, even if the narrator is unaware of them.

There are two basic forms of commentary: explicit and implicit.[8] Explicit commentary is easier to grasp and understand, as it consists of a straightforward message found in the narration. There are three types of explicit commentary that the narrator can make about the story and one about the narration itself:

1. *Interpretation*: The narrator explains the meaning, relevance, or significance of the existents in the storyworld. In Balzac's series of novels *The Human Comedy*, for example, narrators often provide interpretations that contextualise and analyse the social implications of the various behaviours of the characters, almost like a sociologist would do.

2. *Judgement*: The narrator expresses a moral opinion or another form of personal evaluation of the existents in the storyworld. In Henry Fielding's *Tom Jones*, for example, the narrator is constantly giving his opinion about the events and characters of the story, in keeping with his moralising intentions.

---

8 Chatman, pp. 228–60.

3. *Generalisation*: The narrator extrapolates the existents of the story to reach general conclusions about his own world (or the lifeworld of the reader). This is most common in philosophical novels, such as Milan Kundera's *The Unbearable Lightness of Being*, where the narrator comments on the characters and reflects on the events in the novel by connecting them with philosophical notions or events in European history.

4. *Reflection*: The narrator comments on his own narration or other aspects of narrative discourse. This form of self-reflective commentary is already found in early examples of the novel, for instance in Cervantes' *Don Quixote*, where the narrator often pauses to reflect on the task of narrating his story, particularly in the second part of the book, when he feels the need to defend his creation from a plagiariser.

Implicit commentary is a form of irony, a use of discourse to state something different from, or even opposite to, what is actually meant. The irony might be at the expense of the characters or at the expense of the narrator himself. Depending on which levels of narrative it crosses, we can distinguish two basic kinds of implicit commentary in prose fiction:

1. *Ironic narrator*: The narrator makes a statement about the characters or events in the story that means something very different, even the opposite, to what is being stated. Thus, the narrator is being ironic. In this case, the irony is at the expense of the characters in the story but can be understood by the narratee (and eventually, by the reader). A classic example of this form of irony is the first sentence in Jane Austen's *Pride and Prejudice*: 'It is a truth universally acknowledged, that a single man in possession of a good fortune must be in want of a wife.' In fact, the narrator thinks that this is far from being a universal truth, except under the assumptions of a narrow-minded bourgeoisie, as is made clear in the rest of the novel.

2. *Unreliable narrator*: The narrator makes statements that contradict what the implied reader can know (or infer) to be the real intention or meaning of the narrative discourse. In this case, it is the implied author who is being ironic, by communicating indirectly with the implied reader at the expense of the narrator. The narrator in this case is said to be unreliable.[9] In Nikolai Gogol's short story 'Diary of a Madman,' for example, the

---

9   Booth, pp. 149–68.

narrator, a minor civil servant, becomes increasingly unreliable as he descends into madness, making statements whose irony (and comic effect) are only accessible to the implied reader (Fig. 5.5). Another celebrated example of an unreliable narrator is Gulliver in Jonathan Swift's *Gulliver's Travels*, where irony turns into satire, as the gullible narrator tells of his misadventures amongst exotic creatures without ever suspecting that they are meant to ridicule the absurdities and pretensions of human society.

Fig. 5.5 Illustration of Nikolai Gogol's short story 'Diary of a Madman' (1835) by Ilya Repin, Public Domain, https://commons.wikimedia.org/wiki/File:Repin_IE-Illustraciya-Zapiski-sumasshedshego-Gogol_NV4.jpg

Summary

- An element of narrative discourse, narration is the communicative act between a narrator and a narratee that expresses or represents all the existents of the story (characters, events, and environments).

- Narrators (as well as narratees) can be external or internal to the story. Moreover, narrators can speak in the first, second, or third person. And they can narrate events that have already happened, have not yet happened, or are happening at the same time as they are being told.

- When telling a story, narrators can adopt the subjective perspective of one or more of the characters (inward focalisation) or limit themselves to observable events without entering any of the characters' consciousness (outward focalisation).

- Similarly, narrators can know everything about the inner thoughts of characters and the unfolding of events (omniscient), or they can have only partial information about one or more of the characters (limited), or they can only know what can be perceived with the senses (objective).

- Depending on the prominence or degree of involvement of the narrator in the narration, we can distinguish two different narrative methods: telling (summary) and showing (scene).

- Beyond telling and showing, narrators can also make explicit and implicit commentary on the story, sometimes at the expense of characters (ironic narrator) or themselves (unreliable narrator).

References

Booth, Wayne C., *The Rhetoric of Fiction* (Chicago, IL: University of Chicago Press, 1983).

Chatman, Seymour Benjamin, *Story and Discourse: Narrative Structure in Fiction and Film* (Ithaca, NY: Cornell University Press, 2000).

Genette, Gérard, *Narrative Discourse: An Essay in Method* (Ithaca, NY: Cornell University Press, 1990).

Iser, Wolfgang, *The Implied Reader: Patterns of Communication in Prose Fiction from Bunyan to Beckett* (Baltimore, MD: Johns Hopkins University Press, 1995).

Rimmon-Kenan, Shlomith, *Narrative Fiction: Contemporary Poetics* (London, UK: Routledge, 2002), https://doi.org/10.4324/9780203426111

human
foregrounding
storyworld
languages
tropes
some
different
difficult
narrative
ideas
novels
common
world
words
features
say
figurative
about
whole
author
means
used
written
events
literal
symbols
often
metonymy
convey
foregrounded
context
use
environments
things
associated
any
more
new
text
narrator
certain
idea
something
like
translation
even
meaning
read
discourse
language
ordinary
way
dead
metaphor
style
implied
form
real
same
characters
communicate
themselves
order
speak
only
one
other
literature
personification
all
much
many
prose
allegory
literary
while
short
everyday
Fig
novel
example
between
figures
most
generally
story
sometimes
linguistic
original
readers
tenor
reader
stories
speech
texts
devices
vehicle
meanings
fiction
writers

6. Language

If we are speaking about literature, there is no doubt that narrative discourse is made up of language. In fact, the closest we can get to a definition of literature might be to say that it is 'the creative use of language.'[1] Of course, not all stories are told using language. We have already seen (in Chapter 1) that stories can be expressed in many different media, such as comics, dance, or movies. By definition, however, prose fiction narratives are precisely those where a narrator tells a story using words arranged into sentences (see Fig. 6.1).

Fig. 6.1
First page of the Book of Genesis in the Gutenberg Bible, Public Domain, https://de.wikipedia.org/wiki/Gutenberg-Bibel#/media/File:Gutenberg_Bible_B42_Genesis.JPG

---

1 Geoffrey N. Leech, *Language in Literature: Style and Foregrounding* (Harlow, UK: Pearson Longman, 2008), p. 12, https://doi.org/10.4324/9781315846125

The language employed in prose fiction varies widely. Some stories are told in a language that seems common or ordinary, with little use of adjectives and figurative devices, as in Raymond Carver's 'Cathedral' and other minimalist short stories. At the other extreme, some stories are written in a style that is so far removed from everyday language that most readers have a hard time understanding it, as in James Joyce's experimental novel *Finnegans Wake*. This diversity of styles and techniques makes it difficult to describe the language of narrative in any systematic way, short of saying that it is a reflection of the variability of language itself.

The study of language in literature and other forms of discourse has traditionally been the task of rhetoric, an ancient discipline that attempted to understand and teach the art of crafting effective and persuasive discourse. The tradition of rhetoric still influences the analysis and classification of figures of speech and other linguistic devices employed in contemporary prose fiction. In recent times, the application of modern linguistics to the study of literary texts has given rise to stylistics, a discipline that maintains some of the interests and terminology of traditional rhetoric, while incorporating new concerns, concepts, and methodologies.

In this chapter, we will present some key insights about the language of short stories and novels, mostly derived from rhetoric and stylistics, without fleshing out all the linguistic details. To begin with, we need to explain what we mean by style, a characteristic set of linguistic features that is sometimes attributed to the implied author of a story, but also to the real author, or even to a group of authors or to a whole culture. Then, we will discuss the notion of foregrounding, which can help us to identify with more precision the features that distinguish literary from everyday language. Foregrounding in prose fiction can involve different aspects of language, such as the use of figurative devices or figures of speech. After reviewing the most significant of these devices for narrative prose, we will examine the use of symbols and allegory in short stories and novels, an aspect of discourse that brings together language and theme. We will end the chapter by briefly pointing out the importance of literary translation in giving readers access to the rich variety of prose fiction stories written all over the world.

6.1 The Style of Narrative

According to our semiotic model of narrative, discourse is the message that the implied author communicates to the implied reader. This message not only has a content, which is the story, but also a form. The form of discourse is what we generally call its style. In general, the style is a characteristic set of linguistic features associated with a text or group of texts. Thus, the style of a short story or novel is the sum of linguistic features that characterise its narrative discourse.

Narrative style may be attributed to the implied author, which is the virtual entity that enounces the discourse. In this sense, it is generally possible to analyse the linguistic features of style based on the text itself, without any need to know the identity of its real author. In some cases, as in anonymous works or publications under a pseudonym, we might not even have this information. However, we can still identify the specific linguistic features of the text that define its style, or more precisely the style of its implied author. It is in this way that we speak, for example, of the style of *One Thousand and One Nights*, even though it is probably the work of several anonymous compilers.

When we know the identity of the real author of several narratives, we might compare the linguistic features of these works and identify a common style that can be attributed to that author. For example, we speak of the writing style of Jack Kerouac, by comparing the style of novels like *On the Road* or *The Dharma Bums*. Sometimes, we can also identify linguistic features that are shared by texts written in the same genre, or around the same time, or in the same geographic or cultural area, even when the authors are different. In these cases, we may attribute a certain style to a genre (e.g. the style of thrillers), a period (e.g. the style of Romantic novels), or a whole culture (e.g. the style of Korean literature).

Given that short stories and novels are products of modern culture, which is highly individualistic and gives considerable importance to originality and to the creative genius of authors, it is not surprising that style should be associated most of the time with the identity and reputation of a given writer. In such a context, writers themselves often strive to shape (or 'find,' as they sometimes say) their own style, a unique and identifiable set of linguistic features that can raise the literary value of their work.

But style is not just the result of a vain search for literary glory. Authors can be extremely conscious of their use of language, being aware of the crucial importance of choosing the right word, the right turn of phrase, in order to engage the interest and imagination of their readers. Gustave Flaubert, for example, was famously determined to write in the most perfect style, working tirelessly to craft every sentence, every paragraph, sometimes during weeks or months. And although he published some of the most elegant and evocative short stories and novels in the history of literature, with a prose style that has been admired ever since, he always laboured under the impression that his daily battle for perfection could not be won (Fig. 6.2). 'Human language,' says the narrator of *Madame*

Fig. 6.2
Facsimile of the first draft of Gustave Flaubert's short story 'A Simple Heart' (Paris: Edition Conard des Oeuvres Complètes, 1910), Public Domain, https://commons.wikimedia.org/wiki/File:Gustave_Flaubert_-_Trois_Contes,_page_66.jpg

Bovary, 'is like a cracked pot on which we tap crude melodies to make bears dance, while we long to melt the stars.'²

6.2 Foregrounding

As mentioned above, style is the set of linguistic features that characterise a text. Thus, style generally results from multiple and complex decisions about rhythm, phonological patterns, syntactic structure, lexical choice, collocation, paragraph organisation, etc. These decisions are often guided by habit and convention. But they can also involve a variable degree of deviance from established norms and standards. In literature, these deviations are generally more frequent and significant than in other forms of discourse.

A key aspect of literary style is thus the notion of foregrounding. If the language that we use to communicate in everyday situations is taken as the 'norm,' there are many literary texts, including short stories and novels, which tend to deviate from that norm in various ways. Of the specific linguistic features in those texts that diverge from the normal use of language, or from the background, we say that they are foregrounded.

For example, if we wanted to describe the presence of bees in a garden where two people are sitting in silence, we could say something like: 'The silence was interrupted by the buzzing of bees around the plants.' There is nothing extraordinary in this sentence, which simply tries to convey

---

2 Gustave Flaubert, *Madame Bovary: Provincial Manners*, trans. by Margaret Mauldon and Mark Overstall (Oxford, UK: Oxford University Press, 2004), p. 170, my translation.

the intended meaning as economically and effectively as possible. The narrator of Oscar Wilde's *The Picture of Dorian Gray*, however, expresses the same idea very differently: 'The sullen murmur of the bees shouldering their way through the long unmown grass, or circling with monotonous insistence round the dusty gilt horns of the straggling woodbine, seemed to make the stillness more oppressive.'[3] In this long and resonant sentence, which uses many adjectives and figures of speech, the language is foregrounded and brought to the attention of the reader.[4]

The degree of foregrounding in literary texts varies quite considerably. In lyrical poetry, for example, language is usually much more foregrounded than in prose narrative. Short stories and novels, especially the most popular ones, are often written in a style that exhibits few or no perceptible differences from everyday language. But there are also many prose fictions whose language deviates as much as any poem from a supposed norm. Short stories and novels written in prose that uses a highly foregrounded language, reminiscent of lyrical poetry, are sometimes classified as poetic or lyrical prose. Consider, for example, this paragraph from Virginia Woolf's *To the Lighthouse*:

> To want and not to have, sent all up her body a hardness, a hollowness, a strain. And then to want and not to have — to want and want — how that wrung the heart, and wrung it again and again![5]

While foregrounding can be a useful notion to analyse the style of literary texts, it is increasingly difficult to sustain the idea that there is a style-free norm that could serve as background or as a reference to identify the features of literary style. Even when we communicate with each other in everyday situations, our language is not devoid of figures of speech and other linguistic devices that we normally associate with literary language (note, for example, the alliteration in the 'buzzing of bees' of the sentence above). This is particularly the case for metaphors, which are the most significant and widely used figures of speech. Metaphors are commonly employed in prose fiction, but they are also found in ordinary conversation and constitute the most important source of new words and expressions in any language.[6]

Moreover, we should not forget that foregrounding is not just a way of calling attention to language itself, but can serve important functions

---

[3] Oscar Wilde, *The Picture of Dorian Gray*, ed. by Robert Mighall (London, UK: Penguin, 2003), p. 5.

[4] See also Roman Jakobson, 'Linguistics and Poetics', in *Style in Language* (Cambridge, MA: MIT Press, 1960), pp. 350–77, where foregrounding is described in terms of the 'poetic function' of linguistic communication.

[5] Virginia Woolf, *To the Lighthouse*, ed. by Max Bollinger (London, UK: Urban Romantics, 2012), p. 135.

[6] George Lakoff and Mark Johnson, *Metaphors We Live By* (Chicago, IL: University of Chicago Press, 2017).

in narrative and other forms of discourse. In prose fiction, foregrounded language is commonly used in descriptions, when representing characters or environments, and when summarising events. In most ordinary communicative interactions, both the speaker and the listener share a context to which they can refer explicitly or implicitly. In principle, the narrator could also rely on a shared context when telling the story to the narratee. But then many of the details and meanings of the story would be lost to the implied reader, who has no presence at the level of discourse and no direct access to the storyworld. In fact, the existents of the storyworld (events, environments, and characters) only exist insofar as narrative discourse succeeds in representing them in the imagination of the reader. And this can only be done by means of language. In narrative communication, therefore, language is burdened, not only with conveying meaning, but also with recreating the whole context where meaning can emerge in the reader's mind.

In order to succeed in this difficult task, literary discourse needs to use the features of language in slightly different ways than normal discourse tends to do. For example, descriptions in prose fiction often include nouns, adjectives, and phrases that evoke sensory experiences and convey significant details to readers. In summaries and scenes, verbs and adverbs are often carefully selected to recount as precisely and meaningfully as possible the actions of characters and other events in the plot. Moreover, sentences are crafted, not just to communicate events and ideas, but also to affect the rhythm and flow of the narrative. But perhaps the most noticeable rhetorical aspect of literary discourse, common to both short stories and novels, is the widespread use of figurative language to stimulate and engage the reader's imagination.

6.3 Figures of Speech

Figurative language, which includes so-called rhetorical figures, tropes, or figures of speech, is the use of language in ways that deviate from the literal meaning of words and sentences. Literal meaning refers to the precise definition or denotation of words. Figurative meaning, on the other hand, exploits the connotations and associations of words with other words or sounds.

This definition covers a wide array of linguistic features, most of which are part of everyday language, given that we seldom rely exclusively on literal or precise definitions when we communicate with each other. The difference between literary and ordinary language is not that one uses figures of speech while the other one does not. Both literary and ordinary discourse use figurative language, but in literature its use tends to be more intensive and creative than in most other communicative situations, including everyday speech or conversation.

Throughout history, there have been many classifications of figurative devices, which can be found in treatises and textbooks on rhetoric.[7] Here, we will only introduce briefly the most common figures of speech found in narrative discourse, giving some examples drawn from short stories and novels:

1. *Metaphor*: A metaphor establishes a relationship of resemblance between two ideas or things by equating or replacing one (the 'tenor') by the other (the 'vehicle'). Metaphors are usually not created from similarity in denotation (literal meaning), but from some similarity in the connotation of words (their associated or secondary meanings). In Kate Chopin's short story 'The Storm,' for example, the narrator describes the sexual encounter between Alcée and Calixta by saying: 'Her mouth was a fountain of delight.' Of course, she does not mean that there was delight, much less any kind of liquid, gushing out from Calixta's mouth. But the image created by the narrator's metaphor, equating the woman's mouth (tenor) to a fountain (vehicle), allows the reader to understand more vividly the cascade of emotions experienced by Alcée as he kisses his lover. Metaphor is perhaps the most important figure of speech, and many other forms of figurative language can be considered, in a broad sense, metaphorical.

2. *Simile*: Like metaphor, a simile establishes a relationship of resemblance between two ideas or things (tenor and vehicle), but it makes the comparison explicit with a connector (usually, 'like' or 'as'). This connector is not a mere linguistic conjunction, but it allows the simile to specify more clearly the quality or attribute that underlies the comparison between tenor and vehicle. In John Steinbeck's *The Grapes of Wrath*, for example, the narrator describes the landscape with the following words: 'The full green hills are round and soft as breasts.' Here, the hills (tenor) and the breasts (vehicle) are explicitly compared in terms of certain connotative qualities (roundness and softness), but not others (e.g. greenness).

3. *Personification*: A personification attributes personal or human characteristics to a nonhuman entity, object, or idea. In this case, the tenor is not human while the implicit or explicit vehicle is a human-specific quality or attribute. A variant of personification is the attribution of characteristics of animate entities, such as

---

7   For example, Ward Farnsworth, *Farnsworth's Classical English Rhetoric* (Jaffrey, NH: David R Godine, 2016).

nonhuman animals, to inanimate objects or ideas. In Arundhati Roy's *The God of Small Things*, for example, the narrator describes a house (tenor) as if it was an awkwardly dressed person (vehicle): 'The old house on the hill wore its steep, gabled roof pulled over its ears like a low hat.'

4. *Metonymy*: A metonymy replaces an idea or thing by another idea or thing with which it is somehow connected or related in meaning. Unlike metaphor, metonymy does not transfer qualities or attributes from the vehicle to the tenor. In a metonymy, ideas or things are associated because of their contiguity, not their resemblance. The narrator of Louis-Ferdinand Céline's *Journey to the End of the Night*, for example, says: 'When you write, you should put your skin on the table.' Here, the skin is not replacing the writer's self or consciousness based on any resemblance, but because it is contiguous or envelops his body.

5. *Synecdoche*: A synecdoche is a form of metonymy (or at least, closely related with it) where a term for a part refers to the whole of something, or vice versa. In Margaret Mitchell's *Gone with the Wind*, one of the characters says: 'I'm mighty glad Georgia waited till after Christmas before it secedes or it would have ruined the Christmas parties.' The whole state of Georgia is used to refer to its constituents, or rather to its government and legislators. This synecdoche is very common, as we often speak of the actions of a country's government as if they were taken by the whole country.

6. *Hyperbole*: Hyperbole is an exaggeration aimed at emphasising a certain point or creating a strong impression. In Gabriel García Márquez's *One Hundred Years of Solitude*, for example, the narrator introduces the imaginary and primeval world of Macondo with this hyperbolic description: 'The world was so recent that many things lacked names, and in order to indicate them it was necessary to point.'

7. *Oxymoron*: An oxymoron connects or combines elements that appear to be contradictory, but in fact contain a concealed point or a paradox. The narrator of David Foster Wallace's *Infinite Jest*, for example, makes this paradoxical statement: 'That everybody is identical in their secret unspoken belief that way deep down they are different from everyone else.'

All these tropes are routinely used in everyday language, even if they often are not perceived as being figures of speech by speakers or listeners. When a figure of speech has been incorporated into normal language and is no longer recognised as such, we say that it is dead. For example, to say that one has 'fallen in love' (dead metaphor) or that 'time is running out' (dead personification) no longer elicits the kind of surprise, sensory experience, or revelation that literary tropes are supposed to elicit. However, these dead tropes still convey some of their figurative meanings and associations. In general, dead tropes tend to be very good tropes, and this is the reason why they have become so much a part of common language that we do not even notice them anymore.

Other tropes that are also used quite often, both in everyday language and in literary discourse, are clichés. Unlike dead figures of speech, clichés often fail to convey a figurative meaning or create any sensory effect in the reader. Instead, they tend to call attention to themselves, coming across as commonplace and somewhat annoying. Examples of clichés are similes such as 'eyes like stars' or 'teeth like pearls,' which have been so overused in the Western literary tradition that they have lost much of their original force. It is usual, therefore, for critics and rhetoricians to recommend aspiring writers to avoid clichés as much as possible.

In other cases, writers go too far in their efforts to coin new and original tropes and fall into the opposite stylistic blunder. Farfetched tropes or conceits are figures of speech that are too strange, complex, awkward, or extreme to be effective. Like clichés, they tend to call attention to themselves in a negative way. Comparing eyes to 'pearly teeth,' for example, seems like a farfetched image, a conceit that would probably leave the reader baffled and scratching his head.

In figurative language, however, as in all matters of style, there are no hard rules or universally valid prescriptions. At the end of the day, it depends on the readers and the critics to decide whether a trope, no matter how trite or farfetched it may seem, is effective and worthy of praise in the context of a particular narrative discourse.

6.4 Symbolism

In general, a symbol is anything that represents something else by virtue of an arbitrary association.[8] Symbols commonly used by modern humans are traffic signs, words, and flags, amongst many others. Symbols might represent other objects or things, but they can also represent individuals or groups of people, cultures, ideas, beliefs, values, etc. Insofar as human language is a symbolic system, and we also routinely use non-linguistic symbolic systems, there is no doubt that symbols play a crucial role in our understanding of the world and allow us to communicate effectively with each other.

---

8   Charles Sanders Peirce, *Philosophical Writing of Peirce*, ed. by Justus Buchler (New York, NY: Dover Publications, 1955), pp. 102–3.

In narrative discourse, any existent of the story (event, environment, or character) can become a symbol. Sometimes, symbolic associations are expressed by the narrator or by characters in the story, but they can also be left implicit. Some symbols are unequivocally associated with a certain meaning, like the letter 'A' that adulterous women are forced to wear to symbolise their crime in Nathaniel Hawthorne's *The Scarlet Letter*. But there are other symbols whose meaning is open to different interpretations, like the 'night' in Elie Wiesel's novel *Night*, which could be understood to represent, amongst other things, death, Nazism, despair, the loss of faith, or the Holocaust.

Some symbols used in narrative carry their meaning directly from the lifeworld of writers and readers, such as the Christian symbol of the cross. But narratives can also create new symbols, by associating existents of the story with any arbitrary meaning, or give new meanings to symbols that are also used in the lifeworld of readers. For example, the father and son in Cormac McCarthy's novel *The Road* speak about having or carrying 'the fire,' which they conceive as a symbol of goodness and hope as they try to survive in the throes of worldwide annihilation.

Narrative symbols can be internal, when they are associated with other existents of the story. In the Harry Potter series, for example, the scar on Harry's forehead symbolises the connection with his mortal enemy Lord Voldemort, but also marks him as the hero chosen to defeat the evil forces. Symbols can also be external, when the referent is not part of the storyworld, but belongs to the level of discourse or the lifeworld of readers. Again, in Harry Potter, the names of some characters, like Albus Dumbledore, are symbolic to the extent that they refer to meanings in Latin ('albus' means white) or Old English ('dumbledore' means bumblebee) which are only relevant for the implied (or real) reader.

In certain narratives, symbolism becomes the structuring framework of the whole story, turning the events, environments, and characters of the storyworld into representations of something other than themselves, generally moral or abstract ideas. This is what we call an allegory, from the Ancient Greek 'to speak of something else.' Religious myths, like the story of Christ's crucifixion or the life of Buddha, are often constructed as allegories. Beyond their literal meaning, they have a moral and metaphysical significance.

Sometimes, readers will interpret a story as an allegory even if the author did not intend to write it as such. This is called allegoresis, the act of reading any story as allegory. But there are also short stories and novels that are meant to be read as allegories. Narrative discourse is then constructed in such a way that invites readers to find hidden or transcendent meanings in the events, characters, or environments of the storyworld. This kind of sustained symbolism is quite common in fables, parables, and other literary stories that attempt to convey a lesson or illustrate a complex or abstract idea in narrative form.

An example of modern political allegory is George Orwell's *Animal Farm*, a novel about farm animals rebelling against their human owners (Fig. 6.3). While the story can be read literally as a sort of fairytale, it is obvious that the events, characters, and environments of Orwell's imaginary storyworld stand in for the real events, characters, and environments of the Russian Revolution, in order to extract a moral and political lesson about the degeneration of Communist ideals into outright tyranny.

Fig. 6.3
A depiction of a pig dressed as a human capitalist to illustrate George Orwell's *Animal Farm*. By Carl Glover, CC BY 2.0, https://www.flickr.com/photos/34239598@N00/16143409811

6.5 Translation

Prose fiction is written in hundreds of different languages throughout the world. Languages that have the largest share of total speakers (and therefore, writers and readers) tend to be also the languages in which most books are published, although the correlation is far from being exact. At the top of the list, we find languages like English, Chinese, Spanish, French, German, Japanese, or Russian. But there are many other languages with a relatively small number of speakers and yet a considerable number of readers and writers, such as Norwegian, Catalan, or Czech. And there are also widely spoken languages like Malay, Swahili, or Punjabi, whose proportion of writers and publications is comparatively small, but still adds up to a large number in absolute terms.

In such a diverse and globalised world, there is no reader who could possibly be able to read every story in its original language. Even someone with enough proficiency in all major languages of the planet would require at some point or another to rely on translation in order to read prose fiction written in relatively minor or distant languages. Thus, translations play a crucial role in allowing the flow of ideas and stories across different cultures.[9] How many people in China or Japan, for example, have read the original of *Pride and Prejudice* or *Don Quixote*? And how many Europeans have read, or would be able to read, the original of *Romance of the Three Kingdoms* or the *Tale of Genji*? In fact, how many practising Christians around the world have read the Old Testament of the Bible in its original Hebrew version?

But a translation is far from being an exact reproduction of the original text into the target language. Like adaptations, literary translations are always interpretations or rewritings of the original. Even if the translator is successful in faithfully preserving the existents of the story, its narrative discourse is going to be different because it is written in another language. When translating prose fiction, translators need to make difficult linguistic and interpretative choices, balancing their fidelity to the original content and form with the specific requirements and possibilities of the target language. They also need to take into account the expectations of readers in a different language, as well as the rules and conventions prevalent in that culture.

Perhaps the most formidable challenge of literary translation is how to reproduce the style of the original text in the target language. This difficulty tends to increase with the degree of foregrounding of the linguistic features of the text. Thus, translating a popular thriller, such as Dan Brown's *The Da Vinci Code*, into hundreds of languages is a simple operation, which does not require difficult decisions on the part of the various translators involved. On the other hand, translating a lyrical and highly elliptical short story like Yasunari Kawabata's 'The Dancing Girl of Izu,' or a polyphonic modernist novel like Alfred Döblin's *Berlin Alexanderplatz*, with its heavy use of slang and local dialect, can be a daunting task for any translator. This is also the reason why, in general, the translation of poetry tends to be more difficult, and its results more uncertain, than the translation of prose fiction.

In short, literary translation is a creative endeavour, and one that is often unrecognised and undervalued, despite its obvious cultural benefits. While reading a translation is never the same as reading the original, it is the only means for most readers to access the rich and boundless variety of stories that make up 'world literature.'[10]

---

9 Susan Bassnett and André Lefevere, *Constructing Cultures: Essays on Literary Translation* (Clevedon, UK: Multilingual Matters, 1998), pp. 9–10.

10 Johann Wolfgang von Goethe, *Conversations with Eckermann*, trans. by John Oxenford (New York, NY: North Point Press, 1994), p. 132.

Summary

- Style is the characteristic set of linguistic features (rhythm, phonology, syntactic structure, lexical choice, etc.) associated with a text. Style can be attributed to the implied author, but also to the real author, and even to a specific cultural group.

- A key aspect of literary style is foregrounding. In order to effectively communicate the content and meaning of the story and engage the imagination of readers, narrative discourse often relies on foregrounded language, deploying features and devices that diverge from normal or everyday language.

- Figurative language, or the use of figures of speech, including metaphor, simile, personification, metonymy, synecdoche, hyperbole, oxymoron, and others, is a common form of foregrounding in prose fiction.

- Events, environments, and characters in prose fiction become symbols when they represent something other than themselves by virtue of an arbitrary association. When symbolism is sustained throughout the narrative, the story becomes an allegory.

- Despite its complications and limitations, translation is the only means by which most readers can access the rich diversity of short stories and novels published throughout the world.

References

Bassnett, Susan, and André Lefevere, *Constructing Cultures: Essays on Literary Translation* (Clevedon, UK: Multilingual Matters, 1998).

Farnsworth, Ward, *Farnsworth's Classical English Rhetoric* (Jaffrey, NH: David R Godine, 2016).

Flaubert, Gustave, *Madame Bovary: Provincial Manners*, trans. by Margaret Mauldon and Mark Overstall (Oxford, UK: Oxford University Press, 2004).

Goethe, Johann Wolfgang von, *Conversations with Eckermann*, trans. by John Oxenford (New York, NY: North Point Press, 1994).

Jakobson, Roman, 'Linguistics and Poetics,' in *Style in Language* (Cambridge, MA: MIT Press, 1960), pp. 350–77.

Lakoff, George, and Mark Johnson, *Metaphors We Live By* (Chicago, IL: University of Chicago Press, 2017).

Leech, Geoffrey N., *Language in Literature: Style and Foregrounding* (Harlow, UK: Pearson Longman, 2008).

Peirce, Charles Sanders, *Philosophical Writing of Peirce*, ed. by Justus Buchler (New York, NY: Dover Publications, 1955).

Wilde, Oscar, *The Picture of Dorian Gray*, ed. by Robert Mighall (London, UK: Penguin, 2003).

Woolf, Virginia, *To the Lighthouse*, ed. by Max Bollinger (London, UK: Urban Romantics, 2012).

7. Theme

In previous chapters, we have been examining in some detail how prose fiction is constructed and communicated. We have seen how stories are shaped by the arrangement of events into a plot, environments into a setting, and characters into a characterisation. We have also looked at the various ways in which narrative discourse can be articulated in order to effectively communicate stories to the reader, including the process of narration and the use of specific features of language. But we have not yet addressed what is perhaps the most crucial question any reader asks when dealing with a story: *what does it mean?*

At the beginning of this book, we defined narrative as the semiotic representation of a sequence of events, meaningfully connected by time and cause. But what exactly do we mean by 'meaningful'? Are we speaking about the meaning that authors give to the narratives they write, or about the meaning that readers give to the narratives they read? And what happens when these meanings, as they often do, diverge? Should the intention of the author be the standard with which we determine the meaning of a narrative text? Or should we recognise that every reader interprets narrative texts from his or her own perspective, often generating meanings that are at least as valid as those generated by the author?

While literary theory has been asking these questions for a long time,[1] here we are only interested in exploring the elements of meaning that can be identified in narrative discourse, whether they are identified by writers or readers. These elements of meaning are what we call themes. The plural reflects the fact that meanings in fiction are always multiple and changing. A theme, therefore, is simply a meaning identified by an interpreter of narrative discourse. It is important to stress that themes

---

1   For an introduction to these and other debates in literary theory, see Terry Eagleton, *Literary Theory: An Introduction* (Minneapolis, MN: University of Minnesota Press, 2008); Jonathan D. Culler, *Literary Theory: A Very Short Introduction* (Oxford, UK: Oxford University Press, 2011).

© Ignasi Ribó, CC BY 4.0   https://doi.org/10.11647/OBP.0187.07

require some form of interpretation in order to emerge, whether it is the author, a critic, or any other reader who provides such interpretation. It is in this sense that themes connect narrative discourse, and the story conveyed by this discourse, with the lifeworld of readers and writers.

In this final chapter, we will first examine in some detail the concept of theme and we will try to locate its expression in prose fiction. Then we will discuss how narratives often explore themes relating to identity and alterity, particularly in connection with gender and ethnicity. An important notion in the analysis of meaning in narrative is ideology, which encompasses the ideas, values, and beliefs that structure a worldview. As we will see, every narrative is ideological, but ideology can be expressed in different ways in each text. This will lead us to some final considerations regarding the moral and political significance of prose fiction, particularly in the modern world. We will see that some narratives attempt to persuade readers of a moral truth, while others provide a more ambiguous or complex representation of human morality. The function of short stories and novels, as well as other literary texts, has often been the object of passionate discussions. As a conclusion to this textbook, we will consider whether writers should use prose fiction to intervene in society or confine themselves to purely artistic pursuits.

7.1 The Meaning of Narrative

When someone asks what a short story or novel is about, we tend to respond with a synopsis or summary of the plot. The only thing we do in a synopsis is to identify the key existents in the story, including events, environments, and characters, and explain them in our own words. But a synopsis is not a proper answer when someone asks what the story means. In order to respond to this question, we need to identify and give an interpretation of at least one theme in the narrative. Themes are elements of discourse, not of the story. They tell us what the story means, not for the characters in the storyworld, but for anyone who has an interpretative perspective on the story.

Themes are often identified explicitly by narrators when they tell the story and add some form of commentary, whether it is to interpret, judge, generalise, or reflect on the events, environments, and characters of the storyworld (see Chapter 5). While the interpreter in this case is part of narrative discourse, the theme is usually also relevant for the actual readers, who might agree or disagree with the framing of the theme provided by the narrator. In many short stories and novels, especially those with an omniscient narrative voice, the themes explicitly identified by the narrator reflect themes that the author has intentionally introduced into the narrative and to which she is often quite attached. For example, the omniscient narrator of Harriet Beecher Stowe's *Uncle Tom's Cabin* clearly identifies the immorality of slavery as a key theme in the narrative (Fig. 7.1). This conviction is very much at the heart of the author's intention when writing the book, and it has been shared by many of its readers throughout the years.

Fig. 7.1
Harriet Beecher Stowe, *Uncle Tom's Cabin* (Boston: John P. Jewett, 1852), Internet Archive Book Images, Public Domain, https://commons.wikimedia.org/wiki/File:Uncle_Tom%27s_cabin_-_or,_life_among_the_lowly_(1852)_(14586176090).jpg

In many other stories, however, the themes are not explicitly identified. This might be because the narrator refrains from making explicit commentary about the story, for instance when narration is conveyed by an objective narrative voice. One theme in Ernest Hemingway's short story 'Hills Like White Elephants,' for example, seems to be the moral ambiguity of abortion. But this theme is never expressed as such by the narrator, who merely conveys the words and gestures of the couple having a conversation in a forsaken train station, leaving readers to come up with their own interpretations of what it all means.

Similarly, when the narrator is inwardly focalised and has limited knowledge or perspective about the storyworld, his opinions or comments might not reflect the actual themes of the narrative. This is generally the case with unreliable narrators, who are not fully aware of the meaning of the story they are telling. The story of Harper Lee's *To Kill a Mockingbird*, for example, is narrated from the perspective of Scout, a six-year-old girl, who does not understand the meaning of the tragic events she is experiencing. Like *Uncle Tom's Cabin*, one key theme of the book seems to be the immorality of racial inequality. But since the girl is not able to frame or express it, at least not in those terms, this theme can only emerge from the interpretation of readers.

Regarding theme, internal narrators are in a similar position to other characters in the storyworld, the only difference being that at least they know that they are telling a story. Non-narrating characters only exist in the storyworld and take part in the story being told, but they are generally not aware of the story as a story. Thus, unlike the narrator, they are not able to add commentary or give an interpretation of the meaning of events, environments, and characters at the level of narrative discourse. In many cases, however, characters express aspects of theme, in the form of subjective or general reflections about crucial elements of meaning in the story. This is most common in so-called philosophical novels, which often include long dialogues or monologues where characters develop ideas or opinions that connect with the themes of the story. This is the case in Fyodor Dostoyevsky's *The Brothers Karamazov*, for example, where the brothers Ivan and Alyosha engage in a passionate discussion about God and morality, which reveals many of the themes in the novel. And yet, it is only when an external interpreter links these statements with the overall structure of the story that themes begin to emerge.

Finally, themes should not be confused with motifs. If themes are elements of meaning in narrative discourse, motifs are existents that recur throughout the story and often acquire a symbolic significance. For example, in F. Scott Fitzgerald's novel *The Great Gatsby*, the green light that shines at the end of the bay across from Gatsby's mansion is a motif that seems to represent or symbolise his hopes and expectations for the future, and more generally the American dream. Insofar as motifs are usually symbolic, their meaning tends to relate to narrative theme. This is the reason why motifs are sometimes called 'minimal thematic units.'[2] A key theme in *The Great Gatsby* is the decadence and unreality of the American dream; and motifs like the green light serve to reinforce and highlight this theme throughout the narrative.

7.2 Identity

As mentioned at the beginning of this book, narrative is the fundamental way by which we humans make sense of ourselves and our world. Our own identity is little more than a narrative, a story that we tell ourselves and others about who we are, where we come from, and where we are going. But our identity is also constructed by others, as they tell stories about us and place us in the context of social narratives over which we generally have little control or influence. The complex dynamic of identity and alterity, how we construct ourselves, but also how we construct others and how we are constructed by them, is therefore an essential aspect of narrative in all its forms.

---

[2] Gerald Prince, *A Dictionary of Narratology* (Lincoln, NE: University of Nebraska Press, 2003), p. 97.

In modern times, prose fiction has become a privileged vehicle for the construction of individual and collective identities, as well as for the construction of the different others that sustain and demarcate social identification. Only through narrative fiction can we share (or think we share) the subjective experience of another individual, access his or her thoughts, and participate from within in his or her life decisions. This illusion created by fiction is a powerful way to reinforce identification with a given in-group, as well as to approach and try to understand out-groups. But the same illusion can also contribute to distance readers from out-groups that are portrayed in ways that reinforce social stereotypes and negative biases.[3] A crucial theme in many short stories and novels is precisely the social process of defining oneself and others, particularly in relation to two important dimensions of subjectivity: gender and ethnicity.

Gender refers to the set of characteristics that differentiate males and females. Beyond objective characterisations of gender, however, human beings develop their own gender identity based on subjective and social factors. These same factors are often reflected in the themes of short stories and novels, particularly in the depiction of male and female characters and the different roles or psychological traits that narrative discourse assigns to them. As most stories have been written by men, generally from an androcentric perspective, they have tended to cast women in subordinate or dependent roles, often presenting them as ambivalent objects of male desire and repulsion.[4] This construction of the female other in narratives mostly written by males can be seen, for example, in William Thackeray's novel *Vanity Fair*, where women are characterised as either angelic creatures like Emmy Sedley or as dangerous temptresses like Becky Sharp, a dualistic and imaginary representation of femininity that serves to support patriarchal values and discourses.

Before the twentieth century, only a few female writers, such as Charlotte Brontë or George Eliot, had the courage or the opportunity to break social restrictions and conventions in order to produce short stories and novels that represented female subjectivity and agency in their own right, even if they often had to do so by complying with the dominant worldviews of a patriarchal society (see Fig. 7.2). It is only with the development of identity politics that women, as well as other minority groups such as LGBT people, have been able to use prose fiction to openly explore themes of gender identity and sexuality, or simply to speak with their own creative voice about themes that had traditionally been the sole

---

3   On this point, see Chimamanda Ngozi Adichie, 'The Danger of a Single Story' (TED Global, July 2009), https://www.ted.com/talks/chimamanda_adichie_the_danger_of_a_single_story

4   Sandra M. Gilbert and Susan Gubar, *The Madwoman in the Attic: The Woman Writer and the Nineteenth-Century Literary Imagination* (New Haven, CT: Yale University Press, 2000).

Fig. 7.2
'Young Woman Drawing' (1801), oil on canvas by Marie-Denise Villers depicting an independent feminine spirit (possibly a self-portrait), Public Domain, https://commons.wikimedia.org/wiki/File:Villers_Young_Woman_Drawing.jpg

prerogative of heterosexual men. A novel like Doris Lessing's *The Golden Notebook*, for example, mixes personal, professional, literary, political, and feminist themes into a fragmentary narrative that aims to replicate the fragmentation of female consciousness amid social and individual struggles.

Ethnicity is another important theme in modern narrative, as numerous short stories and novels have attempted to reflect on the dynamics of power, oppression, and resistance in the context of colonialism and other interethnic dynamics. We should not forget that prose fiction, at least in its modern form, originates to a large extent in European culture at precisely the same time as Europeans were beginning a worldwide expansion that allowed them to achieve economic, military, and cultural hegemony at the expense of other peoples. Revealing an entrenched ethnocentrism, the European narratives of this period often portray these 'others' as inferior, docile, or underdeveloped, sustaining in more or less explicit terms the colonial project of Western powers.[5] One example of this kind of legitimation can be found in Gustave Flaubert's novel *Salammbô*, whose themes of oriental sensuality, exoticism, and corruption reflect and strengthen a stereotypical and objectifying view of Middle-Eastern and non-European others.

As the process of decolonisation gave way to a postcolonial and globalised world, previously colonised and other non-Western peoples have been struggling to recover their own identity and sense of agency (see Fig. 7.3). And they have often done so by writing stories where they represent themselves as subjects, telling stories with themes that are

---

5   Edward W. Said, *Orientalism* (New York, NY: Vintage Books, 1979).

relevant and meaningful for them, and expressing those themes from their own individual and collective perspective. This is the case, for example, in Chinua Achebe's *Things Fall Apart*, a novel dealing with the destructive consequences of Western colonialism in Africa from the point of view of the colonised.

Fig. 7.3
Mural of Frantz Fanon, author of *The Wretched of the Earth*, Public Domain, https://www.flickr.com/photos/montrealprotest/19582249739

7.3 Ideology

We call ideology the interconnected set of beliefs, ideas, values, and norms that structure the worldview of a person or group. Ideology is generally invisible, especially for the individuals or groups whose views and opinions are largely defined by it. For example, a devout Christian or Buddhist will probably not identify his beliefs as constituting an ideological view of the world, but rather the way things actually are. But all of us are, in one way or another, subject to different ideological positions, whether we adhere to rationalism, liberalism, communism, or other structured systems of thought and value. These ideologies influence to a large extent the meanings we ascribe to ourselves and to everything else in our lifeworld, including other people.

Narrative discourse is particularly effective at communicating ideological views without necessarily stating or even recognising them. If a narrative manages to convince readers that its storyworld is a verisimilar representation of their own lifeworld, the ideology that structures its discourse is likely to be tacitly accepted as a valid and credible one. This is why narratives are often used, consciously or not, to sustain the ideologies of certain social groups, usually those that have more power, or at least the capacity to produce and propagate their discourses more effectively throughout society.[6] At the same time, however, narratives are also used, again, consciously or not, by other groups with less power in society, as they attempt to resist dominant ideologies and express their own set of values and beliefs.

Prose fiction has been, and continues to be, an important vehicle for conveying or contesting ideology, whether explicitly or implicitly. In fact, there is no fiction narrative whose discourse does not express in one way or another at least one ideological position, just as there is no individual or collective opinion that is not ideological. There are four different ways in which ideology can be represented in the narrative discourse of short stories and novels:

1. *Concealed*: Prose fiction can embrace an ideology implicitly, without recognising it as an ideological commitment. Yet, ideology often impregnates the representation of the storyworld (events, environments, characters) or narrative discourse (narration, language, theme). For example, in Ian Fleming's *Casino Royale* and other novels about the secret agent James Bond, everything denotes the masculine, imperialistic, and capitalistic worldview of British elites after the Second World War, from the sports cars Bond drives to the enemies he fights against, the women he seduces, or the language he speaks.

2. *Committed*: Prose fiction can also embrace an ideology explicitly, while trying to convince readers of the truthfulness of its tenets. Socialist realist novels, such as Maxim Gorky's *The Mother*, openly advocate the ideals and values of socialism, by portraying the working class as a heroic agent of political, cultural, and economic transformation towards a better society, against the opposition of self-interested groups like the capitalists or the aristocracy.

3. *Critical*: Prose fiction is sometimes critical of dominant ideologies, without necessarily embracing or committing to an alternative ideology. George Orwell's *1984* (Fig. 7.4), for example, offers a bleak representation of a totalitarian society in a dystopian future, as a way to criticise both the capitalist and socialist ideologies that were struggling for world dominance at the time of the Cold War.

4. *Ambiguous*: Some prose fiction stories present a more ambivalent or ambiguous view of alternative ideological positions. For instance, ideologies can be advocated or symbolised by different characters, as in Thomas Mann's novel *The Magic*

---

6   See Terry Eagleton, *Ideology: An Introduction* (London, UK: Verso, 1991).

Mountain, where the liberal, humanistic, religious, conservative, hedonistic, and nihilistic ideologies prevalent in Europe around the First World War are conveyed through the actions and opinions of various characters in the story. Ideologies can also be represented directly by the events, environments, and characters of an alternative storyworld, as in Ursula K. Le Guin's science-fiction novel *The Dispossessed*, where two different planets, one based on hierarchical capitalism, the other one on authoritarian communism, cooperate and compete with each other in a fictional universe.

Fig. 7.4 Poster depicting Big Brother's slogan from George Orwell's dystopian novel *1984*. By Frederic Guimont, Free Art Licence, https://commons.wikimedia.org/wiki/File:Cropped-big-brother-is-watching-1984.png

7.4 Morality

Some fictional stories try to convey an unambiguous moral message or lesson. We call this message the moral or thesis of the narrative. If there is a thesis, it is always one of the most relevant themes in the narrative. But there might be other themes besides the thesis that the narrative touches upon. The thesis is an aspect of narrative discourse, not of the story. It is an idea, theory, or lesson that the implied author is trying to persuade the implied reader to accept.

A thesis or moral can be explicitly stated in the narrative, but it can also be left implicit. Traditional narrative genres like the fable or parable often have morals, even if these morals are not always explicit. Fables present supernatural characters, often nonhuman animals who act like humans, in order to convey a moral lesson, while parables present ambiguous or puzzling situations and dilemmas in order to provide the lesson in a more roundabout way. These genres were popular in the past, when it was often assumed that literature's main function was to educate readers and provide them with some sort of moral guidance. To a certain extent, this is still the case in modern literature, but the kinds of lessons that narrative and other forms of literary discourse provide today tend to be more ambivalent and controversial.

Novels that have a clear didactic purpose and expound a moral or philosophical message are sometimes called 'thesis novels' (from the French, *'roman à thèse'*). An example of this kind of novel is Voltaire's *Candide*, which tells in a sarcastic tone the story of a young man whose optimistic worldview is repeatedly shaken by the hardships and disasters of the real world.

Fig. 7.5 Oscar Wilde (1884), photographic print on card mount: albume. By Napoleon Sarony, Public Domain, https://commons.wikimedia.org/wiki/File:A_Wilde_time_3.jpg

In general, however, moral lessons in modern prose fiction tend not to constitute the whole theme of the narrative, as in thesis novels. To be sure, there are still modern fictions that explicitly and unambiguously present a moral thesis, especially in children's or popular genres, as in the Harry Potter series. But for the most part, literature is no longer tasked with the education of readers. Rather, it is expected that it will present them with moral or existential alternatives that reflect the complexities and uncertainties of life. Moral lessons, therefore, are often mixed with other themes and ideas, which may even contradict or undermine moral certitude. In Robert Louis Stevenson's novel *The Strange Case of Dr Jekyll and Mr Hyde*, for example, the moral dualism that drives the plot and constitutes the main theme of the narrative is undercut by the realisation that good and evil cannot be easily distinguished from one another, much less decanted as if they were separate essences. In fact, as modern narratives often imply, morality is more a matter of perspective and interpretation, rather than a set of absolute principles or rules that people should follow.

One important consequence of this moral relativism is the modern view that short stories and novels should not refrain from showing what is ugly, unpleasant, improper, or revolting about life and human nature. As one of the characters in Oscar Wilde's *The Portrait of Dorian Gray* says, 'the books that the world calls immoral are books that show the world its own shame' (see Fig. 7.5).[7]

7.5 Art and Politics

A question that has often stirred controversy amongst writers and readers is whether literary narratives should be used as instruments to achieve political and social ends. As we have seen, the idea that narratives, including short stories and novels, have a didactic function is not a modern one. Narratives have traditionally been used to convey moral lessons and worldviews that tended to reflect the ideologies of writers and the societies in which they lived. Even when these ideologies were concealed, instead of being explicitly stated in narrative discourse, they still exercised an influence on readers and had therefore an impact on social and political developments.

Dominant ideologies, when presented as convincing narrative fictions, can make partial worldviews held by specific social groups seem natural and common-sensical. In the past, institutions like slavery, colonialism, or patriarchy, which today are generally considered oppressive and unacceptable, were held as incontrovertible by most reasonable and well-educated people. And narratives reflected those values and ideas, as well as its contestations, in the same way that today's narratives might reflect the values and ideas associated with capitalism, democracy, socialism, multiculturalism, or other ideological positions that occupy current political debates.

What should writers do in relation to these ideas and controversies? Should they use their narratives to intervene in political argument, even to the point of providing a platform to propagate a certain ideology and

---

7   Oscar Wilde, *The Picture of Dorian Gray*, ed. by Robert Mighall (London, UK: Penguin, 2003), p. 208.

persuade readers to embrace it? Or should they refrain from taking a political stance and from trying to convert readers to their cause, while concentrating instead on perfecting their art and writing self-sufficient prose fictions?

Both positions have been defended in modern times by writers and critics who were concerned about this question. For some, like the philosopher Jean-Paul Sartre, author of the novel *Nausea*, writers cannot isolate themselves from reality and have the responsibility to use narratives to express their political commitment in the face of the various forms of exploitation and injustice found in the world. For others, however, a writer should not be bound to any ideology or asked to become the preacher for any cause, no matter how noble or justified it might be. This position is exemplified by Stephen Dedalus, James Joyce's fictional alter ego in his novel *A Portrait of the Artist as a Young Man*, for whom the writer should aim 'to discover the mode of life or of art whereby the spirit can express itself in unfettered freedom.'[8]

At a time when many prose fiction writers are perhaps less motivated by a personal commitment to bring about change in society or by the aspiration to attain beauty or artistic perfection, and rather by the more prosaic goals of entertainment, it might seem idle to ask these questions. But even when authors are not aware of their own motivations or responsibilities, their stories, recreated at every reading by the imagination of countless readers, continue nonetheless to have an impact in the world. Whether prose fiction can contribute to make the world a better place in which to live, helping us to sustain its injustices and immoralities, is still an open question. And perhaps it is one that will remain unanswered as long as we need to tell stories in order to better understand each other.

Summary

- Themes are meanings identifiable in narrative discourse by anyone who has an interpretive perspective on the story, whether it is the narrator, the author, or the reader.

- Many themes in modern prose fiction deal with the dynamics and conflicts of identity (the construction of the self) and alterity (the construction of others), particularly in relation to gender and ethnicity.

- All narratives express some form of ideology — a structured set of values, ideas, and beliefs — whether discourse conceals

---

8   James Joyce, *A Portrait of the Artist as a Young Man* (Oxford: Oxford University Press, 2000), p. 207.

it, commits explicitly to further it, criticises it, or represents it in ambiguous terms.

- Some short stories and novels convey an explicit moral message, or thesis, and attempt to convince readers to accept it, while others might convey more implicit or ambivalent moral lessons.

- It is a matter of some controversy whether prose fiction should contribute to promote social and political ends, or, on the contrary, should be regarded as a purely artistic endeavour, free from external aims.

References

Adichie, Chimamanda N., 'The Danger of a Single Story' (TED Global, July 2009), https://www.ted.com/talks/chimamanda_adichie_the_danger_of_a_single_story

Culler, Jonathan D., *Literary Theory: A Very Short Introduction* (Oxford, UK: Oxford University Press, 2011).

Eagleton, Terry, *Ideology: An Introduction* (London, UK: Verso, 1991).

Eagleton, Terry, *Literary Theory: An Introduction* (Minneapolis, MN: University of Minnesota Press, 2008).

Gilbert, Sandra M., and Susan Gubar, *The Madwoman in the Attic: The Woman Writer and the Nineteenth-Century Literary Imagination* (New Haven, CT: Yale University Press, 2000).

Joyce, James, *A Portrait of the Artist as a Young Man* (Oxford, UK: Oxford University Press, 2000).

Prince, Gerald, *A Dictionary of Narratology* (Lincoln, NE: University of Nebraska Press, 2003).

Said, Edward W., *Orientalism* (New York, NY: Vintage Books, 1979).

Wilde, Oscar, *The Picture of Dorian Gray*, ed. by Robert Mighall (London, UK: Penguin, 2003).

Bibliography

Abbott, H. Porter, *The Cambridge Introduction to Narrative* (Cambridge, UK: Cambridge University Press, 2008), https://doi.org/10.1017/cbo9780511816932

Adichie, Chimamanda N., 'The Danger of a Single Story' (TED Global, July 2009), https://www.ted.com/talks/chimamanda_adichie_the_danger_of_a_single_story

Aristotle, *Poetics*, trans. by Malcolm Heath (London, UK: Penguin Books, 1996).

Bakhtin, Mikhail M., *Problems of Dostoevsky's Poetics*, ed. by Caryl Emerson (Minneapolis, MN: University of Minnesota Press, 1984).

Bakhtin, Mikhail M., *The Dialogic Imagination: Four Essays*, trans. by Michael Holquist and Caryl Emerson (Austin, TX: University of Texas Press, 2011).

Bal, Mieke, *Narratology: Introduction to the Theory of Narrative* (Toronto: University of Toronto Press, 2017).

Barthes, Roland, *The Rustle of Language* (Berkeley, CA: University of California Press, 1989).

Barthes, Roland, 'Introduction to the Structural Analysis of Narrative,' in *A Roland Barthes Reader*, ed. by Susan Sontag, trans. by Stephen Heath (London, UK: Vintage, 1994), pp. 251–95.

Bascom, William, 'The Forms of Folklore: Prose Narratives,' *The Journal of American Folklore*, 78.307 (1965), 3–20.

Bassnett, Susan, and André Lefevere, *Constructing Cultures: Essays on Literary Translation* (Clevedon, UK: Multilingual Matters, 1998).

Bill, Valentine Tschebotarioff, *Chekhov: The Silent Voice of Freedom* (New York, NY: Philosophical Library, 1987).

Booker, Christopher, *The Seven Basic Plots: Why We Tell Stories* (London, UK: Continuum, 2004).

Booth, Wayne C., *The Rhetoric of Fiction* (Chicago, IL: University of Chicago Press, 1983).

Bridgeman, Teresa, 'Time and Space', in *The Cambridge Companion to Narrative*, ed. by David Herman (Cambridge, UK: Cambridge University Press, 2007), pp. 52–65, https://doi.org/10.1017/ccol0521856965

Buchanan, Daniel Crump, *One Hundred Famous Haiku* (Tokyo: Japan Publications, 1973).

Burroway, Janet, *Writing Fiction: A Guide to Narrative Craft* (Chicago, IL: University of Chicago Press, 2019), https://doi.org/10.7208/chicago/9780226616728.001.0001

Chatman, Seymour Benjamin, *Reading Narrative Fiction* (New York, NY: Macmillan, 1993).

Chatman, Seymour Benjamin, *Story and Discourse: Narrative Structure in Fiction and Film* (Ithaca, NY: Cornell University Press, 2000).

Cobley, Paul, *Narrative* (London, UK: Routledge, 2014).

Cohn, Dorrit, *Transparent Minds: Narrative Modes for Presenting Consciousness in Fiction* (Princeton, NJ: Princeton University Press, 1988).

Coleridge, Samuel Taylor, *Biographia Literaria, or, Biographical Sketches of My Literary Life and Opinions*, ed. by James Engell and Walter Jackson Bate (Princeton, NJ: Princeton University Press, 1984).

Culler, Jonathan D., *Literary Theory: A Very Short Introduction* (Oxford, UK: Oxford University Press, 2011).

Eagleton, Terry, *Ideology: An Introduction* (London, UK: Verso, 1991).

Eagleton, Terry, *Literary Theory: An Introduction* (Minneapolis, MN: University of Minnesota Press, 2008).

Eco, Umberto, *The Open Work* (Cambridge, MA: Harvard University Press, 1989).

Farnsworth, Ward, *Farnsworth's Classical English Rhetoric* (Jaffrey, NH: David R Godine, 2016).

Flaubert, Gustave, *Madame Bovary: Provincial Manners*, trans. by Margaret Mauldon and Mark Overstall (Oxford, UK: Oxford University Press, 2004).

Forster, E. M., *Aspects of the Novel* (San Diego, CA: Harcourt Brace Jovanovich, 1985).

Freytag, Gustav, *Freytag's Technique of the Drama: An Exposition of Dramatic Composition and Art*, trans. by Elias J. MacEvan (Charleston, SC: Bibliobazaar, 2009).

Genette, Gérard, *Narrative Discourse: An Essay in Method* (Ithaca, NY: Cornell University Press, 1990).

Gilbert, Sandra M., and Susan Gubar, *The Madwoman in the Attic: The Woman Writer and the Nineteenth-Century Literary Imagination* (New Haven, CT: Yale University Press, 2000).

Goethe, Johann Wolfgang von, *Conversations with Eckermann*, trans. by John Oxenford (New York, NY: North Point Press, 1994).

Greimas, Algirdas Julien, and Joseph Courtés, *Semiotics and Language: An Analytical Dictionary*, trans. by Larry Crist and Daniel Patte (Bloomington, IN: Indiana University Press, 1982).

Herman, David, ed., *The Cambridge Companion to Narrative* (Cambridge, UK: Cambridge University Press, 2007), https://doi.org/10.1017/ccol0521856965

Herman, David, *Basic Elements of Narrative* (Chichester, UK: Wiley-Blackwell, 2009), https://doi.org/10.1002/9781444305920

Herman, David, 'Events and Event-Types,' in *Routledge Encyclopedia of Narrative Theory*, ed. by David Herman, Manfred Jahn, and Marie-Laure Ryan (London, UK: Routledge, 2005), pp. 151–52, https://doi.org/10.4324/9780203932896

Hühn, Peter, ed., *Handbook of Narratology* (New York, NY: Walter de Gruyter, 2009), https://doi.org/10.1515/9783110316469

Iser, Wolfgang, *The Implied Reader: Patterns of Communication in Prose Fiction from Bunyan to Beckett* (Baltimore, MD: Johns Hopkins University Press, 1995).

Jakobson, Roman, 'Linguistics and Poetics', in *Style in Language* (Cambridge, MA: MIT Press, 1960), pp. 350–77.

Johansen, Jørgen Dines, *Literary Discourse: A Semiotic-Pragmatic Approach to Literature* (Toronto, CA: University of Toronto Press, 2002), https://doi.org/10.3138/9781442676725

Joyce, James, *A Portrait of the Artist as a Young Man* (Oxford, UK: Oxford University Press, 2000).

Lakoff, George, and Mark Johnson, *Metaphors We Live By* (Chicago, IL: University of Chicago Press, 2017).

Leech, Geoffrey N., *Language in Literature: Style and Foregrounding* (Harlow, UK: Pearson Longman, 2008), https://doi.org/10.4324/9781315846125

Lodge, David, *The Art of Fiction: Illustrated from Classic and Modern Texts* (New York, NY: Viking, 1993).

Manguel, Alberto, *A History of Reading* (New York, NY: Penguin Books, 2014).

Margolin, Uri, 'Character', in *The Cambridge Companion to Narrative*, ed. by David Herman (Cambridge, UK: Cambridge University Press, 2007), pp. 66–79, https://doi.org/10.1017/ccol0521856965

Margolin, Uri, 'Individuals in Narrative Worlds: An Ontological Perspective,' *Poetics Today*, 11.4 (1990), 843–71

Onega Jaén, Susana, and José Angel García Landa, eds., *Narratology: An Introduction* (London, UK: Routledge, 1996), https://doi.org/10.4324/9781315843018

Page, Norman, *Speech in the English Novel* (London, UK: Macmillan, 1988).

Peirce, Charles Sanders, *Philosophical Writing of Peirce*, ed. by Justus Buchler (New York, NY: Dover Publications, 1955).

Prince, Gerald, *A Dictionary of Narratology* (Lincoln, NE: University of Nebraska Press, 2003).

Rimmon-Kenan, Shlomith, *Narrative Fiction: Contemporary Poetics* (London, UK: Routledge, 2002), https://doi.org/10.4324/9780203426111

Ryan, Marie-Laure, *Possible Worlds, Artificial Intelligence, and Narrative Theory* (Bloomington, IN: Indiana University Press, 1991).

Said, Edward W., *Orientalism* (New York, NY: Vintage Books, 1979).

Sklovskij, Viktor Borisovic, *Theory of Prose* (Elmwood Park, IL: Dalkey Archive Press, 1991).

Stam, Robert, *Film Theory: An Introduction* (Malden, MA: Blackwell, 2000).

Strunk, William, and E. B. White, *The Elements of Style* (Boston, MA: Allyn and Bacon, 1999).

Tuan, Yi-Fu, *Space and Place: The Perspective of Experience* (Minneapolis, MN: University of Minnesota Press, 2011).

Wilde, Oscar, *The Picture of Dorian Gray*, ed. by Robert Mighall (London, UK: Penguin, 2003).

Woolf, Virginia, *To the Lighthouse*, ed. by Max Bollinger (London, UK: Urban Romantics, 2012).

Illustrations

Chapter 1

Fig. 1.1	Collision of Costa Concordia, cropped (2012). By Roberto Vongher, CC BY-SA 3.0, https://commons.wikimedia.org/wiki/File:Collision_of_Costa_Concordia_5_crop.jpg	3
Fig. 1.2	El Ateneo Gran Splendid. A theatre converted into a bookshop. Buenos Aires, Argentina. Photo by Galio, CC BY-SA 3.0, https://commons.wikimedia.org/wiki/File:Buenos_Aires_-_Recoleta_-_El_Ateneo_ex_Grand_Splendid_2.JPG	5
Fig. 1.3	Boccaccio, *Decameron*: 'The Story of the Marchioness of Montferrat,' 15th century. Bibliothèque nationale de France, Public Domain, https://commons.wikimedia.org/wiki/File:Decameron_BNF_MS_Italien_63_f_22v.jpeg	7
Fig. 1.4	Title page of the first edition of Miguel de Cervantes' *Don Quixote* (1605). Biblioteca Digital Hispánica, Public Domain, https://en.wikipedia.org/wiki/Don_Quixote#/media/File:El_ingenioso_hidalgo_don_Quijote_de_la_Mancha.jpg	8
Fig. 1.5	Semiotic model of narrative. By Ignasi Ribó, CC BY.	8
Fig. 1.6	Ernest Hemingway posing for a dust-jacket photo by Lloyd Arnold for the first edition of *For Whom the Bell Tolls* (1940), at Sun Valley Lodge, Idaho, 1939. By Lloyd Arnold, Public Domain, https://en.wikipedia.org/wiki/File:ErnestHemingway.jpg	10
Fig. 1.7	Semiotic model of narrative shown in speech bubbles. By Ignasi Ribó, CC BY.	11

Fig. 1.8	Warner Bros. Studio Tour London: The Making of Harry Potter. Photo by Karen Roe, CC BY 2.0, https://commons.wikimedia.org/wiki/File:The_Making_of_Harry_Potter_29-05-2012_(7528990230).jpg	12

Chapter 2

Fig. 2.1	Bust of Aristotle. Marble Roman copy after a Greek bronze original by Lysippos from 330 BC. Ludovisi Collection, photograph by Jastrow (2006), Public Domain, https://commons.wikimedia.org/wiki/File:Aristotle_Altemps_Inv8575.jpg	18
Fig. 2.2	Diagram showing events interconnected by time only. By Ignasi Ribó, CC BY.	19
Fig. 2.3	Diagram showing events interconnected by time and cause. By Ignasi Ribó, CC BY.	19
Fig. 2.4	Diagram showing events interconnected by time and cause, with the order of events altered by emplotment. By Ignasi Ribó, CC BY.	20
Fig. 2.5	Miniature of St. George and the Dragon, ms. of *Legenda aurea*, Paris (1382). British Library Royal 19 B XVII, f. 109, Public Domain, https://upload.wikimedia.org/wikipedia/commons/e/ef/St_George_Royal19BXVII_109.jpg	21
Fig. 2.6	Title page and portrait of Robinson Crusoe in the first edition of Daniel Defoe's *The Life and Strange Surprizing Adventures of Robinson Crosoe* (1719). British Library, Ambre Troizat, CC BY-SA 4.0, https://upload.wikimedia.org/wikipedia/commons/f/f1/The_life_and_Strange_Surprizing_Adventures_of_Robinson_Crosoe%2C_London%2C_1719.png	23
Fig. 2.7	Illustration of 'Hansel and Gretel' by Arthur Rackham (1909), Public Domain, https://upload.wikimedia.org/wikipedia/commons/d/d1/Hansel-and-gretel-rackham.jpg	24
Fig. 2.8	Oedipus and the Sphinx. Tondo of an Attic red-figure kylix, 480–470 BC. From Vulci. Photograph by Juan José Moral (2009), captured at Museo Gregoriano Etrusco, room XI, Public Domain, https://commons.wikimedia.org/wiki/File:Oidipous_sphinx_MGEt_16541_reconstitution.svg	26
Fig. 2.9	Schema of Freytag's pyramid. By Ignasi Ribó, based on Gustav Freytag, *Freytag's Technique of the Drama: An Exposition of Dramatic Composition and Art*, trans. by Elias J MacEvan (Charleston, SC: Bibliobazaar, 2009), CC BY.	27

Chapter 3

Fig. 3.1	Relationships between existents in the storyworld. By Ignasi Ribó, CC BY.	33
Fig. 3.2	Cover of an early German edition of Franz Kafka's *The Metamorphosis* (*Die Verwandlung*, 1915), Public Domain, https://commons.wikimedia.org/wiki/Category:Kafka_Die_Verwandlung#/media/File:Kafka_Verwandlung_016.jpg	36
Fig. 3.3	Map of Middle Earth, the fantasy world of J. R. R. Tolkien's novels. CC BY-SA 4.0, https://commons.wikimedia.org/wiki/File:World_map_.jpg	38
Fig. 3.4	Pit No. 10 of the Compagnie des mines de Béthune, Nord-Pas-de-Calais, France (ca. 1910), Public Domain, https://commons.wikimedia.org/wiki/File:Sains-en-Gohelle_-_Fosse_n%C2%B0_10_-_10_bis_des_mines_de_B%C3%A9thune_(B).jpg	39
Fig. 3.5	Hogwarts Castle in the ride *Harry Potter and the Forbidden Journey* at The Wizarding World of Harry Potter, Universal Studios Islands of Adventure Orlando, Florida. Source: Marcos Becerra, CC BY 2.0, https://www.flickr.com/photos/mbecerra/6402825573	41
Fig. 3.6	'The Art of Painting' (1666–1668), oil on canvas by Jan Vermeer, Public Domain, https://commons.wikimedia.org/wiki/File:Jan_Vermeer_-_The_Art_of_Painting_-_Google_Art_Project.jpg	42
Fig. 3.7	Drawing of a wall barometer, Public Domain, https://pixabay.com/p-1297523	43
Fig. 3.8	Schema of verisimilitude in fiction and nonfiction. By Ignasi Ribó, CC BY.	44

Chapter 4

Fig. 4.1	Illustration of Lewis Carroll *Alice in Wonderland* (1865). By John Tenniel, Public Domain, https://en.wikipedia.org/wiki/Alice%27s_Adventures_in_Wonderland#/media/File:Alice_par_John_Tenniel_02.png	48
Fig. 4.2	Fan art representing Lord Voldemort and Nagini, from the Harry Potter saga, made with charcoal, acrylics and watercolours. By Mademoiselle Ortie aka Elodie Tihange, CC BY 4.0, https://fr.wikipedia.org/wiki/Fichier:Lord_Voldemort.jpg	52

Fig. 4.3	'Madame Hessel en robe rouge lisant' (1905), oil on cardboard. By Édouard Vuillard, Public Domain, https://commons.wikimedia.org/wiki/File:%C3%89douard_Vuillard_-_Madame_Hessel_en_robe_rouge_lisant_(1905).jpg	53
Fig. 4.4	'Don Quixote and Sancho Panza at a crossroad,' oil on canvas. By Wilhelm Marstrand (1810–1873), CC0 1.0, https://commons.wikimedia.org/wiki/File:Wilhelm_Marstrand,_Don_Quixote_og_Sancho_Panza_ved_en_skillevej,_uden_datering_(efter_1847),_0119NMK,_Nivaagaards_Malerisamling.jpg	53
Fig. 4.5	Warner Bros. Studio Tour, London: The Making of Harry Potter. Source: Karen Roe, CC BY 2.0, https://commons.wikimedia.org/wiki/File:The_Making_of_Harry_Potter_29-05-2012_(7358054268).jpg	55
Fig. 4.6	'Man without Qualities n°2' (2005), oil and metal on canvas. By Erik Pevernagie, CC BY-SA 4.0, https://commons.wikimedia.org/wiki/File:Man_without_Qualities_n%C2%B02.jpg	56
Fig. 4.7	Portrait of Fyodor Dostoevsky by Vasily Petrov (1872). Tretyakov Gallery, Public Domain, https://commons.wikimedia.org/wiki/Фёдор_Михайлович_Достоевский#/media/File:Dostoevsky_1872.jpg	61

Chapter 5

Fig. 5.1	Édouard Frédéric Wilhelm Richter, *Scheherazade* (before 1913), Public Domain, https://commons.wikimedia.org/wiki/File:Edouard_Frederic_Wilhelm_Richter_-_Scheherazade.jpg	67
Fig. 5.2	First-edition cover of *The Catcher in the Rye* (1951) by J. D. Salinger, Public Domain, https://commons.wikimedia.org/wiki/File:The_Catcher_in_the_Rye_(1951,_first_edition_cover).jpg	69
Fig. 5.3	Promotional still from the 1941 film *The Maltese Falcon*, published in the *National Board of Review Magazine*, p. 12, Public Domain, https://commons.wikimedia.org/wiki/File:Maltese-Falcon-Tell-the-Truth-1941.jpg	73
Fig. 5.4	Theatre scene: two women making a call on a witch (all three of them wear theatre masks). Roman mosaic from the Villa del Cicerone in Pompeii, now in the Museo Archeologico Nazionale (Naples). By Dioscorides of Samos, Public Domain, https://commons.wikimedia.org/wiki/File:Pompeii_-_Villa_del_Cicerone_-_Mosaic_-_MAN.jpg	75

Fig. 5.5	Illustration of Nikolai Gogol's short story 'Diary of a Madman' (1835) by Ilya Repin, Public Domain, https://commons.wikimedia.org/wiki/File:Repin_IE-Illustraciya-Zapiski-sumasshedshego-Gogol_NV4.jpg	78

Chapter 6

Fig. 6.1	First page of the Book of Genesis in the Gutenberg Bible, Public Domain, https://de.wikipedia.org/wiki/Gutenberg-Bibel#/media/File:Gutenberg_Bible_B42_Genesis.JPG	81
Fig. 6.2	Facsimile of the first draft of Gustave Flaubert's short story 'A Simple Heart' (Paris: Edition Conard des Oeuvres Complètes, 1910), Public Domain, https://commons.wikimedia.org/wiki/File:Gustave_Flaubert_-_Trois_Contes,_page_66.jpg	84
Fig. 6.3	A depiction of a pig dressed as a human capitalist to illustrate George Orwell's *Animal Farm*. By Carl Glover, CC BY 2.0, https://www.flickr.com/photos/34239598@N00/16143409811	91

Chapter 7

Fig. 7.1	Harriet Beecher Stowe, *Uncle Tom's Cabin* (Boston: John P. Jewett, 1852), Internet Archive Book Images, Public Domain, https://commons.wikimedia.org/wiki/File:Uncle_Tom%27s_cabin_-_or,_life_among_the_lowly_(1852)_(14586176090).jpg	97
Fig. 7.2	'Young Woman Drawing' (1801), oil on canvas by Marie-Denise Villers depicting an independent feminine spirit (possibly a self-portrait), Public Domain, https://commons.wikimedia.org/wiki/File:Villers_Young_Woman_Drawing.jpg	100
Fig. 7.3	Mural of Frantz Fanon, author of *The Wretched of the Earth*, Public Domain, https://www.flickr.com/photos/montrealprotest/19582249739	101
Fig. 7.4	Poster depicting Big Brother's slogan from George Orwell's dystopian novel *1984*. By Frederic Guimont, Free Art Licence, https://commons.wikimedia.org/wiki/File:Cropped-big-brother-is-watching-1984.png	103
Fig. 7.5	Oscar Wilde (1884), photographic print on card mount: albume. By Napoleon Sarony, Public Domain, https://commons.wikimedia.org/wiki/File:A_Wilde_time_3.jpg	104

Examples of Short Stories and Novels

The following extracts from Wikipedia provide a brief summary of the short stories and novels cited as examples throughout the textbook. The Wikipedia texts have been modified, expanded, or adapted as needed. Hyperlinks to the full entries are given in order to help students find additional information and references about these narratives in the course of their own research.

– A –

1984 (1949) by George Orwell: A dystopian novel set in a world of perpetual war, omnipresent government surveillance, and public manipulation by a totalitarian party and its leader, Big Brother. The novel tells the story of a party member who becomes disaffected and is prosecuted as a thought criminal by the repressive state apparatus. https://en.wikipedia.org/wiki/Nineteen_Eighty-Four

2001: A Space Odyssey (1968) by Arthur C. Clarke: A science-fiction novel, written in parallel with the film of the same name directed by Stanley Kubrick. It narrates a voyage to Jupiter of a human crew with the sentient computer Hal after the discovery of a mysterious black monolith affecting human evolution. https://en.wikipedia.org/wiki/2001:_A_Space_Odyssey_(novel)

Alice's Adventures in Wonderland (1865) by Lewis Carroll: A novel about a girl named Alice who falls down a rabbit hole into a fantasy world populated by peculiar, anthropomorphic creatures. https://en.wikipedia.org/wiki/Alice%27s_Adventures_in_Wonderland

The Ambassadors (1903) by Henry James: A novel that follows the trip of protagonist Lewis Lambert Strether to Europe in pursuit of Chad Newsome, his widowed fiancée's supposedly wayward son. The third-person narrative is told exclusively from Strether's point of view. https://en.wikipedia.org/wiki/The_Ambassadors

Animal Farm (1945) by George Orwell: A political allegory about a farm where animals revolt against their human owners only to become enslaved and exploited by the pigs, who establish a new system as oppressive and tyrannical as the previous one. https://en.wikipedia.org/wiki/Animal_Farm

Anna Karenina (1878) by Leo Tolstoy: A Russian novel narrating the tragic story of a married aristocrat/socialite and her extramarital affair with the affluent Count Vronsky. It is regarded as one of the most accomplished realist novels. https://en.wikipedia.org/wiki/Anna_Karenina

Around the World in Eighty Days (1873) by Jules Verne: An adventure novel narrating the story of the English aristocrat Phileas Fogg and his newly employed French valet Passepartout, as they attempt to circumnavigate the world in 80 days on a £20,000 wager set by his friends at the Reform Club. https://en.wikipedia.org/wiki/Around_the_World_in_Eighty_Days

– B –

Berlin Alexanderplatz (1929) by Alfred Döblin: A modernist novel narrating, through montage and multiple points of view, the story of Franz Biberkopf, a convicted murderer who comes out from prison and struggles to survive in the underworld of Berlin during the interwar years. https://en.wikipedia.org/wiki/Berlin_Alexanderplatz

Bible: A collection of sacred texts or scriptures that Jews and Christians consider to be a product of divine inspiration and a record of the relationship between God and humans. It contains texts from different authors and epochs, including narratives, songs, codes, chronicles, proverbs, letters, and other writings. https://en.wikipedia.org/wiki/Bible

Blanquerna (ca. 1283) by Ramon Llull: A medieval novel chronicling the life of the eponymous hero, a nobleman who follows his religious vocation and is eventually elected as Pope. It is a major work of literature written in Catalan and one of the earliest predecessors of the modern European novel. https://en.wikipedia.org/wiki/Blanquerna

Bridget Jones's Diary (1996) by Helen Fielding: A novel written in the form of a personal diary chronicling a year in the life of Bridget Jones, a thirty-something single working woman living in London. https://en.wikipedia.org/wiki/Bridget_Jones%27s_Diary

The Brothers Karamazov (1879–1880) by Fyodor Dostoyevsky: A philosophical novel set in nineteenth-century Russia dealing with ethical debates about God, free will, and morality. It is a spiritual drama of moral struggles concerning faith, doubt, judgment, and reason, set against a modernising Russia, with a plot that revolves around the subject of patricide. https://en.wikipedia.org/wiki/The_Brothers_Karamazov

– C –

Candide (1759) by Voltaire: A satirical novella that tells the story of a young man, Candide, who grows up being indoctrinated with an optimistic philosophy by his mentor, until he is confronted with the reality of hardship and suffering in the world. https://en.wikipedia.org/wiki/Candide

Casino Royale (1953) by Ian Fleming: The first in the James Bond series of spy novels, it begins with the British secret agent gambling at the casino in Royale-les-Eaux to bankrupt Le Chiffre, the treasurer of a French union and a member of the Russian secret service. https://en.wikipedia.org/wiki/Casino_Royale_(novel)

The Catcher in the Rye (1951) by J. D. Salinger: A novel in which Holden Caulfield, a teenager from New York City, describes events that took place in December 1949, when he was trying to deal with his feelings of anguish and alienation from society. https://en.wikipedia.org/wiki/The_Catcher_in_the_Rye

'*Cathedral*' (1983) by Raymond Carver: A short story narrating the unwelcome visit of a blind friend of the narrator's wife for dinner. https://en.wikipedia.org/wiki/Cathedral_(short_story)

'*A Christmas Carol*' (1843) by Charles Dickens: A novella that tells the story of Ebenezer Scrooge, an elderly miser who, after being visited by the ghost of his former business partner and the spirits of Christmas Past, Present and Yet to Come, is transformed into a kinder, gentler man. https://en.wikipedia.org/wiki/A_Christmas_Carol

The Counterfeiters (1925) by André Gide: A novel with many characters and crisscrossing plotlines, which revolve around the distinction of the original versus its copy. It is a novel-within-a-novel, with Édouard, the alter ego of Gide, intending to write a book of the same title. https://en.wikipedia.org/wiki/The_Counterfeiters_(novel)

Crime and Punishment (1866) by Fyodor Dostoyevsky: A Russian novel about the mental anguish and moral dilemmas of Rodion Raskolnikov, an impoverished ex-student in Saint Petersburg who kills an unscrupulous pawnbroker for her money. https://en.wikipedia.org/wiki/Crime_and_Punishment

– D –

'The Dancing Girl of Izu' (1926) by Yasunari Kawabata: A lyrical and elegiac short story narrating the infatuation of a Tokyo student with a young dancing girl during a brief encounter with her family of itinerant performers on the Izu Peninsula. https://en.wikipedia.org/wiki/The_Dancing_Girl_of_Izu

Daphnis and Chloe (2nd century) by Longus: An Ancient Greek pastoral novel that tells the love story and adventures of a couple of young shepherds. It is one of the most ancient predecessors of the modern novel. https://en.wikipedia.org/wiki/Daphnis_and_Chloe

The Da Vinci Code (2003) by Dan Brown: A thriller novel that follows an American symbologist after a murder in the Louvre Museum in Paris, when he becomes involved in a battle between powerful enemies over a religious mystery. https://en.wikipedia.org/wiki/The_Da_Vinci_Code

The Decameron (1353) by Giovanni Bocaccio: A collection of *novelle* (short stories) told by a group of young men and women sheltering in a secluded villa just outside Florence to escape the Black Death. https://en.wikipedia.org/wiki/The_Decameron

The Dharma Bums (1958) by Jack Kerouac: A novel narrating the protagonist's search for meaning on his trip across the Western United States. The book had a significant influence on the hippie counterculture of the 1960s. https://en.wikipedia.org/wiki/The_Dharma_Bums

'Diary of a Madman' (1835) by Nikolai Gogol: A short story presented as the personal diary of a minor civil servant in Russia during the repressive era of Nicholas I, as he descends into insanity. https://en.wikipedia.org/wiki/Diary_of_a_Madman_(short_story)

The Dispossessed: An Ambiguous Utopia (1974) by Ursula K. Le Guin: A utopian science-fiction novel set in two different planets divided into several states and dominated by two political and military rivals, one with a capitalist economy and patriarchal system and the other with an authoritarian system that claims to rule in the name of the proletariat. https://en.wikipedia.org/wiki/The_Dispossessed

Don Quixote (1605–1615) by Miguel de Cervantes: Generally considered the first and one of the greatest modern novels, it tells the story of a middle-aged impoverished country squire who, deluded by his readings of chivalric romances, recruits a simple farmer, Sancho Panza, and sets out to revive chivalry, undo wrongs and bring justice to the world under the name of Don Quixote de la Mancha. https://en.wikipedia.org/wiki/Don_Quixote

Dubliners (1914) by James Joyce: A collection of fifteen short stories that form a naturalistic depiction of Irish middle-class life in and around Dublin in the early years of the twentieth century. https://en.wikipedia.org/wiki/Dubliners

– F –

The Fall (1956) by Albert Camus: A philosophical novel consisting of a series of dramatic monologues in which the protagonist, Jean-Baptiste Clamence, reflects upon his life to a stranger. https://en.wikipedia.org/wiki/The_Fall_(Camus_novel)

'The Fall of the House of Usher' (1839) by Edgar Allan Poe: A short story and a gothic mystery that begins with the unnamed narrator arriving at the crumbling house of his friend, Roderick Usher, after receiving a letter from him. https://en.wikipedia.org/wiki/The_Fall_of_the_House_of_Usher

Finnegans Wake (1939) by James Joyce: An avant-garde novel, considered one of the most difficult works of fiction in the English language. The entire book is written in a largely idiosyncratic language, which blends standard English lexical items and neologistic multilingual puns and portmanteau words to unique effect. https://en.wikipedia.org/wiki/Finnegans_Wake

'Funes the Memorious' (1942) by Jorge Luís Borges: A short story, included in the anthology *Ficciones*, telling the story of Ireneo Funes, a man who acquires a prodigious memory after suffering a head injury and can remember every single detail of his experiences. https://en.wikipedia.org/wiki/Funes_the_Memorious

– G –

Germinal (1885) by Émile Zola: A naturalistic novel narrating the story of a young migrant worker who arrives at the forbidding coal mining town of Montsou in the far north of France to earn a living as a miner. https://en.wikipedia.org/wiki/Germinal_(novel)

The God of Small Things (1997) by Arundhati Roy: A novel about the childhood experiences of fraternal twins whose lives are destroyed by social constraints and obligations. https://en.wikipedia.org/wiki/The_God_of_Small_Things

The Golden Ass (ca. 170) by Lucius Apuleius: Also known as *The Metamorphoses*, this Ancient Roman novel tells the story of Lucius, who accidentally turns himself into an ass while practicing magic and sets out on a long journey, literal and metaphorical, to recover his human form. It is the only Ancient Roman novel in Latin to survive in its entirety. https://en.wikipedia.org/wiki/The_Golden_Ass

The Golden Notebook (1962) by Doris Lessing: A novel telling the story of writer Anna Wulf through fragments of her notebooks that intermingle different aspects of her personal, political, and life experiences and reflections. https://en.wikipedia.org/wiki/The_Golden_Notebook

Gone with the Wind (1936) by Margaret Mitchell: A novel narrating the struggles of young Scarlett O'Hara, the spoiled daughter of a well-to-do plantation owner in Georgia, who must use every means at her disposal to claw her way out of poverty following the defeat of the Confederates in the Civil War. https://en.wikipedia.org/wiki/Gone_with_the_Wind_(novel)

The Grapes of Wrath (1939) by John Steinbeck: A novel telling the story of the Joads, a poor family of tenant farmers driven from their Oklahoma home by drought, economic hardship, agricultural industry changes, and bank foreclosures during the Great Depression. https://en.wikipedia.org/wiki/The_Grapes_of_Wrath

Great Expectations (1861) by Charles Dickens: A novel that depicts the personal growth and development of an orphan nicknamed Pip, as he tries to escape poverty in the midst of England's industrial expansion. https://en.wikipedia.org/wiki/Great_Expectations

The Great Gatsby (1925) by F. Scott Fitzgerald: A novel about the young and mysterious millionaire Jay Gatsby and his quixotic passion and obsession for the beautiful former debutante Daisy Buchanan, set on prosperous Long Island in the summer of 1922. https://en.wikipedia.org/wiki/The_Great_Gatsby

Gulliver's Travels (1726) by Jonathan Swift: A satirical novel narrating the adventures of Lemuel Gulliver, as he is repeatedly shipwrecked in distant and imaginary lands, inhabited by civilisations and creatures that ridicule aspects of human nature and society. https://en.wikipedia.org/wiki/Gulliver%27s_Travels

– H –

'Hansel and Gretel' (1812) by the Brothers Grimm: A German fairy tale that recounts the ordeal of a young brother and sister kidnapped by a cannibalistic witch living in a forest house built of candy. https://en.wikipedia.org/wiki/Hansel_and_Gretel

Harry Potter and the Philosopher's Stone (1997) by J. K. Rowling: The first novel in the Harry Potter series, it tells the story of a young wizard who discovers his magical heritage as he makes close friends and a few enemies in his first year at Hogwarts School of Witchcraft and Wizardry. https://en.wikipedia.org/wiki/Harry_Potter_and_the_Philosopher%27s_Stone

Heart of Darkness (1899) by Joseph Conrad: A novella that tells the story of Marlow's obsession with the ivory trader Kurtz, as he sets out to find him in the most remote parts of the Congo River basin. https://en.wikipedia.org/wiki/Heart_of_Darkness

'Hills Like White Elephants' (1927) by Ernest Hemingway: A short story focusing on a conversation between an American man and a woman at a Spanish train station while waiting for a train to Madrid. https://en.wikipedia.org/wiki/Hills_Like_White_Elephants

The Hobbit (1937) by J. R. R. Tolkien: A children's fantasy novel that narrates the quest of Bilbo Baggins, a home-loving hobbit, together with the wizard Gandalf and a party of thirteen dwarves, who set out to recover the treasure guarded by Smaug the dragon. https://en.wikipedia.org/wiki/The_Hobbit

The Human Comedy (1830–1850) by Honoré de Balzac: *La Comédie humaine* is a multi-volume collection of interlinked novels and stories depicting French society during the Restoration (1815–1830) and the July Monarchy (1830–1848), including such novels as *Père Goriot* or *Lost Illusions*, amongst many others. https://en.wikipedia.org/wiki/La_Com%C3%A9die_humaine

– I –

If on a Winter's Night a Traveller (1979) by Italo Calvino: A postmodern novel framed by a story about the reader trying to read a book with the same title as the novel. https://en.wikipedia.org/wiki/If_on_a_winter%27s_night_a_traveler

Iliad (ca. 750 BC) by Homer: An Ancient Greek epic poem set during the Trojan War, the ten-year siege of the city of Troy by a coalition of Greek states. It tells of the battles and events that took place during the weeks that were dominated by a quarrel between King Agamemnon and the warrior Achilles. It is the most influential work of ancient literature in the Western tradition. https://en.wikipedia.org/wiki/Iliad

Infinite Jest (1996) by David Foster Wallace: A complex and multifaceted postmodern novel centred on a junior tennis academy and a nearby substance-abuse recovery centre, touching with humour and melancholy on many topics, including addiction and recovery, suicide, family relationships, entertainment and advertising, film theory, and tennis. https://en.wikipedia.org/wiki/Infinite_Jest

In Search of Lost Time (1913–1927) by Marcel Proust: A novel in seven volumes that follows the narrator's recollections of childhood and experiences into adulthood during late-nineteenth-century to early-twentieth-century upper-class France. https://en.wikipedia.org/wiki/In_Search_of_Lost_Time

I, Robot (1950) by Isaac Asimov: A collection of science-fiction short stories sharing a common narrative frame and the theme of the interaction between humans and robots. https://en.wikipedia.org/wiki/I,_Robot

– J –

Jane Eyre (1847) by Charlotte Bronte: An English novel narrating the emotions and experiences of its eponymous heroine, including her growth to adulthood and her love for Mr Rochester. https://en.wikipedia.org/wiki/Jane_Eyre

Journey to the End of the Night (1932) by Louis-Ferdinand Céline: A philosophical novel narrating the experiences of antihero Ferdinand Bardamu during the First World War, and his subsequent life in colonial Africa, his experience of the rise of American capitalism, and his time spent in bourgeois France, while expressing a nihilistic and cynical view of human nature, institutions, and society. https://en.wikipedia.org/wiki/Journey_to_the_End_of_the_Night

– K –

'The Killers' (1927) by Ernest Hemingway: A short story about a pair of criminals who enter a restaurant seeking to kill a boxer, who is hiding out for unknown reasons. Hemingway's minimalist use of an objective narrator in this story was highly influential. https://en.wikipedia.org/wiki/The_Killers_(Hemingway_short_story)

– L –

Les Liaisons dangereuses (1782) by Pierre Chordelos de Laclos: An epistolary novel telling the story of the Marquise de Merteuil and the Vicomte de Valmont, two rivals (and ex-lovers) who use seduction as a weapon to socially control and exploit others, all the while enjoying their cruel games and boasting about their manipulative talents. https://en.wikipedia.org/wiki/Les_Liaisons_dangereuses

Lolita (1955) by Vladimir Nabokov: A novel that narrates the obsession and sexual relationship of Humbert Humbert, a middle-aged literature professor, with a twelve-year-old girl, Dolores Haze, after contriving to become her stepfather. https://en.wikipedia.org/wiki/Lolita

The Lord of the Rings (1954–1955) by J. R. R. Tolkien: An epic fantasy novel that tells the story of a party constituted of a few hobbits, two men, a dwarf, an elf, and a wizard, as they set out on a difficult journey through Middle Earth with the aim of destroying the ring that could give absolute power to the Dark Lord Sauron. https://en.wikipedia.org/wiki/The_Lord_of_the_Rings

– M –

Madame Bovary (1856) by Gustave Flaubert: A French novel narrating the story of Emma Bovary, the wife of a doctor who has adulterous affairs and lives beyond her means in order to escape the banalities and emptiness of provincial life. It is considered one of the masterpieces of realist narrative in literature. https://en.wikipedia.org/wiki/Madame_Bovary

The Magic Mountain (1924) by Thomas Mann: A novel telling the story of Hans Castorp, who undertakes a journey to visit his tubercular cousin in a sanatorium in Davos, high up in the Swiss Alps, and ends up staying there for seven years, until the First World War concludes. https://en.wikipedia.org/wiki/The_Magic_Mountain

The Maltese Falcon (1929) by Dashiell Hammett: A detective novel about a beautiful young woman who hires Sam Spade to find her missing sister, who supposedly ran off with a crook, and gets him involved in the search for the jewel-encrusted statuette of a falcon. https://en.wikipedia.org/wiki/The_Maltese_Falcon_(novel)

The Man Without Qualities (1930–1943) by Robert Musil: An unfinished modernist novel in three volumes and various drafts considered to be one of the most significant European novels of the twentieth century. The novel takes place during the last days of the Austro-Hungarian monarchy, and has a winding plot that often veers into allegorical and ironical dissections on a wide range of existential themes concerning humanity, society, culture, and identity. https://en.wikipedia.org/wiki/The_Man_Without_Qualities

The Metamorphosis (1915) by Franz Kafka: A novella written in German that narrates the awkward and agonising experience of Gregor Samsa, a travelling salesman, who wakes up to find himself transformed into a giant insect and becomes estranged from his own family. https://en.wikipedia.org/wiki/The_Metamorphosis

Moby Dick (1851) by Herman Melville: An adventure novel telling the story of the obsessive quest of Ahab, captain of a whaler, to take revenge on Moby Dick, the white whale that, on a previous whaling voyage, bit off Ahab's leg at the knee. https://en.wikipedia.org/wiki/Moby-Dick

The Mother (1906) by Maxim Gorky: A socialist realist novel, portraying the life of a woman who works in a Russian factory doing hard manual labour and fighting poverty and hunger among other hardships, in the midst of revolutionary unrest. https://en.wikipedia.org/wiki/The_Mother_(Gorky_novel)

Mrs Dalloway (1925) by Virginia Woolf: A modernist novel narrating a day in the life of Clarissa Dalloway, a fictional upper-class woman in post-First-World-War England. https://en.wikipedia.org/wiki/Mrs_Dalloway

– N –

Nausea (1938) by Jean-Paul Sartre: An existentialist novel about a dejected historian who experiences with a sense of nausea how reality encroaches on his intellectual and spiritual freedom. https://en.wikipedia.org/wiki/Nausea_(novel)

Night (1960) by Elie Wiesel: A novel based on the author's experience with his father in the Nazi German concentration camps at Auschwitz and Buchenwald in 1944–1945, toward the end of Second World War. https://en.wikipedia.org/wiki/Night_(book)

– O –

Odyssey (ca. 750 BC) by Homer: An Ancient Greek epic poem attributed to Homer. Partly a sequel to the *Iliad*, it tells of the hazardous return home to Ithaca of the war hero Odysseus (known as Ulysses in Roman myths)

after the fall of Troy. It is one of the most influential works of literature in the Western tradition. https://en.wikipedia.org/wiki/Odyssey

Oedipus Rex (429 BC) by Sophocles: An Athenian tragedy widely regarded as the masterpiece of the genre. It dramatises the story of Oedipus, who has become king of Thebes while unwittingly fulfilling a prophecy that he would kill his father, Laius (the previous king), and marry his mother, Jocasta. https://en.wikipedia.org/wiki/Oedipus_Rex

The Old Man and the Sea (1952) by Ernest Hemingway: A novella that tells the story of an epic battle between an aging, experienced fisherman, Santiago, and a large marlin near the coast of Cuba. https://en.wikipedia.org/wiki/The_Old_Man_and_the_Sea

One Hundred Years of Solitude (1967) by Gabriel García Márquez: A novel telling the story of several generations of the Buendía family, whose patriarch, José Arcadio Buendía, founds the town of Macondo, in the metaphoric country of Colombia. The magical realist style and thematic substance of the novel established it as an important representative of the Latin American literary boom of the 1960s and 1970s. https://en.wikipedia.org/wiki/One_Hundred_Years_of_Solitude

One Thousand and One Nights (medieval): A collection of Middle-Eastern folk tales compiled in Arabic during the Islamic Golden Age and framed by the story of a sultan and his wife Scheherazade, who succeeds in remaining alive thanks to her storytelling. Some of the stories in the book have become widely known around the world, such as 'Ali Baba and the Forty Thieves,' 'Sindbad the Sailor,' or 'Aladdin and the Magic Lamp.' https://en.wikipedia.org/wiki/One_Thousand_and_One_Nights

On the Road (1957) by Jack Kerouac: A novel narrating the travels across the United States of two countercultural characters, who try to live as intensely as possible against a backdrop of jazz, poetry, and drug use. It is considered the most significant literary work of the Beat generation. https://en.wikipedia.org/wiki/On_the_Road

– P –

Pale Fire (1966) by Vladimir Nabokov: A novel presented as a 999-line poem titled 'Pale Fire,' written by the fictional poet John Shade, with a foreword and lengthy commentary written by Shade's neighbour and academic colleague, Charles Kinbote. https://en.wikipedia.org/wiki/Pale_Fire

The Picture of Dorian Gray (1890) by Oscar Wilde: A philosophical novel about a handsome young man who makes a Faustian bargain that allows him to pursue a hedonistic and libertine life and stay always young and beautiful, while his portrait ages and records all of his excesses. https://en.wikipedia.org/wiki/The_Picture_of_Dorian_Gray

A Portrait of the Artist as a Young Man (1916) by James Joyce: A novel tracing the religious and intellectual awakening of young Stephen Dedalus, a fictional alter ego of Joyce, as he questions and rebels against the Catholic and Irish conventions under which he has grown, culminating in his self-exile from Ireland. https://en.wikipedia.org/wiki/A_Portrait_of_the_Artist_as_a_Young_Man

Pride and Prejudice (1813) by Jane Austen: A romance novel that narrates the emotional development of the protagonist, Elizabeth Bennet, who learns the error of making hasty judgements and comes to appreciate the difference between the superficial and the essential. https://en.wikipedia.org/wiki/Pride_and_Prejudice

– R –

The Red and the Black (1830) by Stendhal: A historical psychological novel chronicling the attempts of a provincial young man to rise socially beyond his modest upbringing through a combination of talent, hard work, deception, and hypocrisy. The title refers to the tension between the clerical (black) and secular (red) interests of the protagonist. https://en.wikipedia.org/wiki/The_Red_and_the_Black

'A Report to an Academy' (1917) by Franz Kafka: A short story in the form of a conference given by an ape named Red Peter, who tells his scientific audience how he learned to behave like a civilised human and how he has been affected by this transformation. https://en.wikipedia.org/wiki/A_Report_to_an_Academy

The Road (2006) by Cormac McCarthy: A post-apocalyptic short novel telling the journey of a father and his young son over a period of several months, across a landscape blasted by an unspecified cataclysm that has destroyed most of life and civilisation. https://en.wikipedia.org/wiki/The_Road

Robinson Crusoe (1719) by Daniel Defoe: A novel presented as an autobiography by the eponymous character, a castaway who spends twenty-eight years on a remote tropical desert island near Trinidad, encountering cannibals, captives, and mutineers, before ultimately being rescued. https://en.wikipedia.org/wiki/Robinson_Crusoe

Romance of the Three Kingdoms (ca. 1321) by Luo Guanzhong: Historical novel set in the turbulent years towards the end of the Han dynasty and the Three Kingdoms period in Chinese history. It tells the story, in part historical, in part legendary and mythical, of the feudal lords and their retainers, who tried to replace the dwindling Han dynasty or to restore it. https://en.wikipedia.org/wiki/Romance_of_the_Three_Kingdoms

– S –

Salammbô (1862) by Gustave Flaubert: A historical novel set in Carthage during the 3rd century BC, immediately before and during the Mercenary Revolt which took place shortly after the First Punic War. https://en.wikipedia.org/wiki/Salammb%C3%B4

'A Scandal in Bohemia' (1891) by Arthur Conan Doyle: The first short story featuring the fictional detective Sherlock Holmes, who is engaged in solving a mystery involving European royalty. https://en.wikipedia.org/wiki/A_Scandal_in_Bohemia

The Scarlet Letter (1850) by Nathaniel Hawthorne: A historical novel telling the story of Hester Prynne, who conceives a daughter from an adulterous affair and struggles to create a new life of repentance and dignity in the context of a seventeenth-century Puritan colony in Massachusetts. https://en.wikipedia.org/wiki/The_Scarlet_Letter

Second Thoughts (1957) by Michel Butor: A novel written in the second person telling the story of a middle-aged man who takes the train from Paris to Rome to visit his lover, whom he has not informed of his arrival. https://en.wikipedia.org/wiki/Second_Thoughts_(Butor_novel)

Sense and Sensibility (1811) by Jane Austen: A novel that narrates the life and romantic vicissitudes of the three Dashwood sisters as they move with their widowed mother from their family home. https://en.wikipedia.org/wiki/Sense_and_Sensibility

'A Simple Heart' (1877) by Gustave Flaubert: A short story about an innocent and loyal peasant girl named Félicité who picks up work in a widow's house as a servant. https://en.wikipedia.org/wiki/Three_Tales_(Flaubert)#.22A_Simple_Heart.22

'The Snows of Kilimanjaro' (1936) by Ernest Hemingway: A short story narrating the last moments and bitter memories of a writer who has been fatally injured while on a safari in Africa. https://en.wikipedia.org/wiki/The_Snows_of_Kilimanjaro_(short_story)

A Song of Ice and Fire (1996-) by George R. R. Martin: An unfinished (at the time of writing) series of epic fantasy novels narrating the conflicts between rival kingdoms in the fictional continents of Westeros and Essos. https://en.wikipedia.org/wiki/A_Song_of_Ice_and_Fire

The Sorrows of Young Werther (1774) by Johann Wolfgang von Goethe: A loosely autobiographical novel, presented as a collection of letters written by Werther, a young artist who falls in love with Charlotte, a beautiful girl engaged to another man. It is one of the most influential novels of the Romantic movement in literature. https://en.wikipedia.org/wiki/The_Sorrows_of_Young_Werther

The Sound and the Fury (1929) by William Faulkner: A novel narrating thirty years in the life of the Compson family, former Southern aristocrats who are struggling to deal with the dissolution of their family and its reputation. https://en.wikipedia.org/wiki/The_Sound_and_the_Fury

'**The Storm**' (1898) by Kate Chopin: A short story narrating the sexual affair between a married man and a married woman during a storm in nineteenth century Louisiana. https://en.wikipedia.org/wiki/The_Storm_(short_story)

Strange Case of Dr Jekyll and Mr Hyde (1886) by Robert Louis Stevenson: A gothic mystery novella about a London lawyer who investigates the relationship between his old and reputable friend, Dr Henry Jekyll, and the evil Edward Hyde. https://en.wikipedia.org/wiki/Strange_Case_of_Dr_Jekyll_and_Mr_Hyde

– T –

Tale of Genji (1010) by Murasaki Shikibu: A psychological novel recounting the life of Hikaru Genji, the son of an ancient Japanese emperor and a low-ranking concubine, while describing the customs of the aristocratic society of the Heian period. It is considered the earliest predecessor of the modern novel in the Eastern tradition. https://en.wikipedia.org/wiki/The_Tale_of_Genji

'**The Tell-Tale Heart**' (1843) by Edgar Allan Poe: A short story told by an unnamed narrator who attempts to demonstrate his sanity, while describing a murder he committed. https://en.wikipedia.org/wiki/The_Tell-Tale_Heart

Things Fall Apart (1958) by Chinua Achebe: A novel depicting pre- and post-colonial life in late-nineteenth-century Nigeria through the life of

Okonkwo, an Igbo leader and local wrestling champion in the fictional village of Umuofia. https://en.wikipedia.org/wiki/Things_Fall_Apart

To Kill a Mockingbird (1960) by Harper Lee: A novel narrating three years in the life of six-year-old Scout Finch at the time of the arrest and trial of a young black man accused of raping a white woman in a small town of Alabama during the Great Depression. https://en.wikipedia.org/wiki/To_Kill_a_Mockingbird

Tom Jones (1749) by Henry Fielding: A comic morality tale that narrates the life of Tom Jones in order to explore human nature and the contrast between virtue and evil in human society. https://en.wikipedia.org/wiki/The_History_of_Tom_Jones,_a_Foundling

To the Lighthouse (1927) by Virginia Woolf: A modernist novel centred on the Ramsay family and their visits to the Isle of Skye in Scotland between 1910 and 1920. https://en.wikipedia.org/wiki/To_the_Lighthouse

Tristram Shandy (1759–1767) by Laurence Sterne: *The Life and Opinions of Tristram Shandy, Gentleman* is a novel purporting to be the autobiography of the eponymous character. Its style, marked by digression, double entendre, and graphic devices, has been highly influential amongst modernist and postmodernist authors. https://en.wikipedia.org/wiki/The_Life_and_Opinions_of_Tristram_Shandy,_Gentleman

– U –

Ulysses (1922) by James Joyce: A novel that chronicles an ordinary day in the life of Leopold Bloom in Dublin. The novel is constructed as an ironic parallel to Homer's epic poem *Odyssey*. It is one of the most influential works of modernist literature. https://en.wikipedia.org/wiki/Ulysses_(novel)

The Unbearable Lightness of Being (1984) by Milan Kundera: A philosophical novel that narrates the lives of two women, two men, and a dog, while exploring the artistic and intellectual life of Czech society from the Prague Spring of 1968 to the invasion of Czechoslovakia by the Soviet Union and its aftermath. https://en.wikipedia.org/wiki/The_Unbearable_Lightness_of_Being

Uncle Tom's Cabin; or, Life among the Lowly (1852) by Harriet Beecher Stowe: A novel depicting the brutality and immorality of slavery in the southern United States, which pleads for Christian love to overcome cruelty. A bestseller at the time, the novel helped to further the abolitionist cause. https://en.wikipedia.org/wiki/Uncle_Tom%27s_Cabin

The Unnamable (1953) by Samuel Beckett: A modernist novel consisting entirely of a disjointed monologue from the perspective of an unnamed and immobile protagonist. https://en.wikipedia.org/wiki/The_Unnamable_(novel)

– V –

Vanity Fair (1847–1848) by William Thackeray: A novel that follows the lives of Becky Sharp and Emmy Sedley amid their friends and families during and after the Napoleonic Wars. https://en.wikipedia.org/wiki/Vanity_Fair_(novel)

The Virgin Suicides (1993) by Jeffrey Eugenides: A novel written in the first person plural from the perspective of an anonymous group of teenage boys who struggle to find an explanation for the deaths of five sisters. https://en.wikipedia.org/wiki/The_Virgin_Suicides

– W –

War and Peace (1869) by Leo Tolstoy: A novel that chronicles the history of the French invasion of Russia and the impact of the Napoleonic era on Tsarist society through the stories of five Russian aristocratic families. It is regarded as a central work of Russian literature and one of Tolstoy's finest literary achievements. https://en.wikipedia.org/wiki/War_and_Peace

Glossary of Narrative Terms

– A –

Adaptation: A work based on a story previously told in a different medium.

Agency: The capacity to act in an environment.

Agon: Ancient Greek term for conflict, particularly the conflict found in tragedy.

Allegory: A story that uses extended symbolism in order to communicate meanings, generally moral or abstract ideas, beyond the literal meaning of events, environments, and characters.

Antagonist: A character in the story that opposes the protagonist and struggles to frustrate his or her goals.

Archetype: A type that has become part of the psychology and culture of a society and appears in many different storyworlds.

Atmosphere: The quality of an environment that reflects meaningful relationships between things and events or characters.

– B –

Biography: A narrative of a person's life.

– C –

Character: An entity with agency in a storyworld.

Characterisation: The meaningful arrangement or presentation of the characters of the story.

Chronotope: The configuration of time and space in language and narrative discourse.

Cliché: A figure of speech that has been so overused that it has lost much of its original force and is perceived in negative terms.

Climax: Stage in the evolution of a plot in which the conflict achieves its maximum intensity and decisive events take place.

Collaborative fiction: A form of writing where two or more authors share creative control of the narrative.

Commentary: Any pronouncement of the narrator that goes beyond a description or account of the existents of the storyworld.

Conceit (also, **Farfetched trope**): A figure of speech that seems too strange, complex, awkward, or extreme to be effective, and tends to call attention to itself, often in a negative way.

Conflict: Clash of two opposing wills or goals, sometimes (but not always) resulting in violent confrontation.

– D –

Dead trope: A figure of speech that has been incorporated into normal language and is no longer recognised as such.

Description: The textual representation of characters or environments.

Dialogism: The use in narrative of different perspectives or viewpoints, whose interaction or contradiction is important to the story's interpretation.

Dialogue: Representation of verbal or speech interactions between characters, often accompanied by dialogue or speech tags.

Dialogue tags (also, **Speech tags**): Narrative indications that often accompany dialogue in prose fiction to provide information about the speakers, the quality and tone of speech, the environment, etc.

Discourse: The means through which a narrative is communicated by the implied author to the implied reader.

– E –

Embedded narration: A story that is narrated within another story.

Emplotment: The arrangement of the events of the story into a plot.

Environment: Everything that surrounds the characters in the storyworld.

Epiphany: A sudden and life-changing moment of illumination that provides a new understanding of the world to the characters.

Event: A change of state occurring in the storyworld, including actions undertaken by characters and anything that happens to a character or its environment.

Exposition: Initial stage in the evolution of a plot where the setting and the characters are introduced.

External narrator or narratee: A narrator or narratee who is a figure of discourse but not an existent of the storyworld.

– F –

Falling action: Stage in the evolution of a plot where the conflict unravels and wanes, as it begins to move towards a resolution.

Farfetched trope: See **Conceit**.

Fiction: A narrative that represents imagined (or partially imagined) characters, events, and environments.

Figurative language: See **Figure of speech**.

Figure of speech (also, **Figurative language**, **Rhetorical device**, **Trope**): The use of language in ways that deviate from the literal meaning of words and sentences, exploiting connotations and associations with other words or sounds.

Flashback: The presentation at some point in the plot of a previous event from the story.

Flashforward: The presentation at some point in the plot of a future event from the story.

Focalisation: The perspective or point of view adopted by the narrator when telling the story.

Foregrounding: A set of linguistic features of discourse that deviate from the normal or ordinary use of language.

Foreshadowing: Anticipation of future events through hints given earlier in the plot.

– G –

Genre: Conventional grouping of texts (or other semiotic representations) based on certain shared features.

– H –

Hyperbole: A figure of speech that makes an exaggerated claim in order to emphasise a certain point or create a strong impression.

– I –

Ideology: An interconnected set of beliefs, ideas, values, and norms that structures the worldview of a person or group.

Implied author: The projection of the real author in the text, as can be inferred by the reader from the text itself.

Implied reader: The virtual reader to whom the implied author addresses its narrative, and whose thoughts and attitudes may differ from an actual reader.

Individuation: The ascription of mental, physical, or behavioural properties (characteristics) to a character.

In medias res: A Latin expression that refers to narratives that begin at some point in the middle of the plot ('in the middle of things').

Internal narrator or narratee: A narrator or narratee who, besides being a figure of discourse, is also an existent of the storyworld, particularly a minor or major character.

Inward focalisation: Narration from the subjective perspective or point of view of one or more focal characters.

Irony: Use of discourse to state something different from, or even opposite to, what is meant.

Ironic narrator: A narrator who makes statements about the characters or events in the story that mean something very different, even the opposite, of what is being stated.

– L –

Lifeworld: The world experienced by writers and readers in their lives.

Limited narrator: A narrator who has only limited knowledge about the internal or psychological states of one or some of the existents in the storyworld.

– M –

Metaphor: A figure of speech that establishes a relationship of resemblance between two ideas or things by equating or replacing one with the other.

Metonymy: A figure of speech that replaces an idea or thing with another idea or thing, with which it is somehow connected or related in meaning.

Mise en abyme (from French, 'placed into an abyss'): A literary device that embeds self-reflecting or recursive images to create paradoxical narrations.

Moral: See **Thesis**.

Motif: An existent that recurs throughout the story and often has a symbolic significance.

– N –

Narratee: The figure of discourse to whom a story is told by the narrator.

Narrative: Semiotic representation of a sequence of events, meaningfully connected by time and cause.

Narratology: The systematic study of narratives in order to understand their structure (how they work) and function (what they are for).

Narrator: The figure of discourse that tells the story to a narratee.

Nonfiction: A narrative that claims to represent characters, events, and environments drawn from the lifeworld of writers and readers.

Novel: A fictional narrative of book length, written in prose, and generally intended to be read in silence.

Novella: A fictional narrative longer than a short story but shorter than a standard novel, written in prose, and generally intended to be read in silence.

– O –

Objective narrator: A narrator who has no knowledge about the internal or psychological states of any of the characters in the storyworld and can only report what can be observed from the outside.

Omniscient narrator: A narrator who knows everything about the existents of the storyworld, including the internal or psychological states of all characters and the unfolding of events.

Outward focalisation: Narration that avoids taking the subjective perspective or point of view of any of the characters.

Oxymoron: A figure of speech that connects or combines elements that appear to be contradictory, but which contain a concealed point or a paradox.

– P –

Personification: A figure of speech that attributes personal or human characteristics to a nonhuman entity, object, or idea.

Plot: The meaningful arrangement or representation of the events in the story in a temporal and causal sequence.

Polyphony: The inclusion in narrative of a diversity of points of view and voices.

Prose: Written or spoken language without metrical structure.

Protagonist: The main character of a story, the one who struggles to achieve some goal.

– R –

Realism: Narrative discourse that aims to construct a storyworld that is an accurate reflection of the lifeworld (i.e. the 'real' world).

Red herring: Foreshadowing of an event that never takes place in the plot.

Resolution: The action of solving a conflict at the end of the plot.

Rhetoric: The art of crafting effective or persuasive discourse.

Rhetorical device: See **Figure of speech**.

Rising action: Stage in the evolution of a plot where the conflict becomes complex and increases in intensity.

– S –

Scene: The narrative representation of an environment, set of characters, and sequence of events in enough detail to create the illusion that the events are unfolding in front of the narratee (and ultimately, the reader).

Semiotics: Study of meaning-making processes, especially the use of signs and signifying systems to communicate meanings.

Setting: The meaningful arrangement or representation of the environments in the story.

Short story: A fictional narrative of shorter length than a novel and a novella, written in prose, and generally intended to be read in silence.

Showing: The direct representation of the events, environments, and characters of a story without the intervention (or, in the case of narrative showing, with minimal or limited intervention) of a narrator.

Significant detail: A descriptive detail that reveals meaningful connections between the existents of the story and helps the reader to recreate the storyworld in her imagination.

Simile: A figure of speech that establishes a relationship of resemblance between two ideas or things through an explicit comparison using a connector (usually, 'like' or 'as').

Speech tags: See **Dialogue tags**.

Story: A complete chronological sequence of interconnected events.

Storyworld: The world of the story, which includes different types of existents (events, environments, and characters).

Style: A characteristic set of linguistic features associated with a text or group of texts.

Summary: The narrative representation of events by compressing their duration.

Surprise: A turn of the plot that disproves the reader's anticipation of events.

Suspense: Reader's anticipation and curiosity about future plot developments based on previous events.

Symbol: Anything that represents something else by virtue of an arbitrary association. In narrative, symbols are existents of the story that become arbitrarily associated with internal or external meanings.

Synecdoche: A figure of speech, closely related with metonymy, where a term for a part refers to the whole of something, or vice versa.

Synopsis: A brief summary of the events, environments, and characters of a story.

– T –

Telling: The representation of a story through the mediation of a narrator, who gives an account and often interprets or comments on the events, environments, or characters of the storyworld.

Theme: A relevant meaning identified by an interpreter in narrative discourse.

Thesis (also, **Moral**): A message or lesson explicitly or implicitly conveyed by narrative discourse.

Topography: The arrangement of natural and artificial things laid out in space.

Trope: See **Figure of speech**.

Type: See **Typical character**.

Typical character (also, **Type**): A character that represents a particular aspect of humanity or a particular group of humans.

– U –

Universal character: A character that represents a general aspect of humanity or the whole human species.

Unreliable narrator: A narrator who makes statements that contradict what the implied reader knows (or infers) to be the real intention or meaning of the narrative discourse.

– V –

Verisimilitude: Features of narrative discourse that attempt to convince readers that the storyworld is a faithful imitation of the 'real' world.

Verse: Written or spoken language arranged in metrical rhythm, and often containing a rhyme.

This book need not end here...

Share

All our books—including the one you have just read—are free to access online so that students, researchers and members of the public who can't afford a printed edition will have access to the same ideas. This title will be accessed online by hundreds of readers each month across the globe: why not share the link so that someone you know is one of them?

This book and additional content is available at:
https://doi.org/10.11647/OBP.0187

Customise

Personalise your copy of this book or design new books using OBP and third-party material. Take chapters or whole books from our published list and make a special edition, a new anthology or an illuminating coursepack. Each customised edition will be produced as a paperback and a downloadable PDF.

Find out more at:
https://www.openbookpublishers.com/section/59/1

You may also be interested in:

The Classic Short Story, 1870-1925
Theory of a Genre
Florence Goyet

https://doi.org/10.11647/OBP.0039

Whose Book is it Anyway?
A View From Elsewhere on Publishing, Copyright and Creativity
Edited by Janis Jefferies and Sarah Kember

https://doi.org/10.11647/OBP.0159

Hyperion, or the Hermit in Greece
Friedrich Hölderlin. Translated by Howard Gaskill

https://doi.org/10.11647/OBP.0160

www.ingramcontent.com/pod-product-compliance
Lightning Source LLC
Chambersburg PA
CBHW041241240426
43668CB00023B/2450